D1433325

The New Manual of Kung Fu

The new manual of Kung Fu

by Peter P. Tang

ARCO PUBLISHING COMPANY, INC.
New York

Published 1976 by Arco Publishing Company, Inc.
219 Park Avenue South, New York, N.Y. 10003
Copyright © 1975 by Peter P. Tang
All rights reserved
Library of Congress Catalog Card Number 75–13890
ISBN 0–668–03851–9

Printed in Great Britain

Dedicated To My Father
and The Memory Of My Mother

獻給父親

紀念母親

Contents

Preface 9
To the teach-yourself student 10
To the kung-fu-class student 11
To the teacher 11

Basic Positions 13
The Fist 13
The Fist Edge 14
The Hand 14
The Spear Hand 15
The Hook 15
The Horse Stance 15
The Bow-Arrow Stance 16
The Free Stance 16
The L Stance 17
The Ball of the Foot 17
Vulnerable Points of the Body 18

Sequence 1 19
Part 1 20
Part 2 24
Part 3 28
Part 4 31

Sequence 2 35
Part 1 36
Part 2 40
Part 3 41
Part 4 48

Sequence 3 53
Part 1 54
Part 2 59
Part 3 64
Part 4 72

Power 80
The iron hand 80
Reasons for hand training 80
Reasons against hand training 81
Reasons against heavy conditioning
of the hand 81
The Tang method 81
Equipment 82
The Palm 84
The Palm heel 84
Edge of hand 84
Back of hand 85
Finger tips 85
Fist edge 85
Fist back 86
Fist front 86
Medication 87
The Time Machine 87
Edge of hand against Palm heel 88
Palm heel against Palm heel 88
Knuckles against knuckles 89
Fist edge against fist front 90
Hand exercise 90
Break testing 92

Force and Motion 98
How we learn 98
Forces acting in a straight line 98
Resolution of forces 101
Centre of gravity 103
Stability and Balance 105
The law of inertia 108
The law of acceleration 108
The law of interaction 108

Preface

MARTIAL ARTS is a unique Chinese cultural inheritance. Kung Fu is the technique and expression of Martial Arts. This wealth of experience has been accumulated over thousands of years out of war and human conflict. The ancient Chinese studied, experimented, invented and improved many skills. Many schools of Martial Arts have thus been founded, each characterised by its own style and pattern; all are effective and powerful. Kung Fu is receiving growing attention in the West.

This book is concerned with that discipline of Martial Arts called the 'Art of Fisticuffs' (Chuan Shu 拳 術). It is the art of 'open-hand' fighting, employing a series of movements of attacks and parries, counter-attacks and blocks, without the use of weapons. It is not like boxing in the West. In this discipline, there are two main schools, the SHAOLIN (少 林) and the TAI CHI (太 極). Shaolin is the name of the monastery in the province of Honan, where a famous Budhist monk named Bodhidharma developed the first

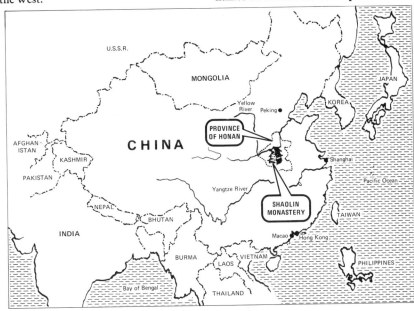

18 exercises for strengthening the physical constitution of the body. This happened in the 6th century AD. Since then, these 18 toughening exercises were further developed and perfected by the monks who also taught them to Buddhist believers. Kung Fu was born and grew.

At a time which was marked by nomadic, warring tribes it became essential for defence against attack and was further refined into a system with a military bias—Martial Arts.

Although Buddhism had been known in China since the 1st century AD it was not until the 6th century AD that it began to grow in influence and rival the existing philosophical and religious doctrine Taoism. The principles of Buddhism are the relief of suffering and kindness to all living things. It was natural therefore that the Buddhists should be interested in health and to increase the numbers of their followers, they made great use of medicine. They translated many important Indian medical works and brought Indian cultural values to China.

Thus, in the practice of respiratory exercises, there are yogic elements. These exercises can purify the heart and calm the spirit. Therefore, medicine and Kung Fu had become twins, born of the same mother. No wonder Kung Fu is reinforced by its therapeutic value.

In the 12th century AD, General Yo Fei of the Sung dynasty together with the monk Chiao Yuan built up a system of 173 series of movements. These movements bear a certain resemblance to the Japanese karate.

Tai Chi is a very old term meaning the Highest above. This Highness exists in two forms, the Yin and the Yang. Yin means negative which refers to all matters dark, cold or feminine. Yang means positive for all matters light, warm or masculine. The interaction of these two forms creates all phenomena of the world.

The Tai Chi School of Fisticuffs created a system in which the yin and yang must be balanced. This means that a person's mind, sense organs, internal organs and movements of the limbs must be in equilibrium. The method to achieve

The inseparable of yin-yang symbols

this is to perform a sequence of slow movements involving breathing control. The results of this practice are the promotion of the player's general physique, the increase of resistance against diseases, longevity and an effective measure of self-defence. To present a sequence of this school would need a separate volume and is therefore not included in this book.

This book is designed for beginners of both sexes, the young and the grown up, who may have no previous knowledge of this Art. Obviously, Kung Fu is a powerful means of self-defence. Furthermore, it develops and consolidates personal strength, speed, sensitivity and endurance. Therefore, Kung Fu is also a powerful way of keeping fit. Regular practice will promote good health, both in the body and the mind. Many students, now at the age of seventy or eighty, are finding themselves still fit and lively, active and happy, enjoying life to the full, as the consequence of years of practice.

To the teach-yourself student

The fact that you cannot join a Kung Fu class because such a class does not exist within your locality, or because of other reasons, does not mean that you can not learn Kung Fu. This book provides you with your own course. By following the 3 sequences carefully and patiently, you will be able to acquire enough skill to reach a first grade standard. This means that you will be in the position of defending yourself when absolutely necessary and of keeping yourself fit.

There is one suggestion that will help

you along greatly. If you can find a friend or two, a brother or sister, to practise with you, by all means do so. You will find the lessons becoming so much more exciting and interesting and you will enjoy the company. What's more, you can help one another to interpret the photographs and to understand the instructions. You will spot one another's mistakes and correct them. Two heads are better than one. Inspiration will flow in. Regular sessions may be arranged. Remember that it is much better to practise regularly rather than intensely for one period and then stop for a long time. You will need a fair-size room or the garden.

When you read this book, the book faces you. The demonstrator in the photographs also faces you. His right is your left and his left is your right. When he moves in one direction, you are supposed to move in the opposite direction. This makes it difficult for you to follow his movements. One simple way to overcome this difficulty is that you put the book alongside you. Both you and the book should face the same direction or the same wall of the room. Then you can follow the movements more easily.

The 3 sequences should be thoroughly learned and practised. Each movement follows the other in a smooth continuous sequence. You should be able to execute them automatically and without hesitation, so that, in the case of defence, part of the sequences can be instantly and subconsciously picked out and applied to any particular situation.

The chapter on *Force and Motion* is a scientific study of their theory and application to Kung Fu. It is interesting and inspiring. With understanding, it will enhance your appreciation of the skills which you are learning. At later stages, you may even be able to invent your own movements.

To the Kung Fu class student

Now you can have this book to keep as your own, to refer to anytime you want. Read the preceding paragraphs under the heading 'To the teach-yourself student'. They apply just as much to you.

This book consolidates your learning in class and ensures that you progress steadily and rapidly. A good start is essential. With these extra sequences which give you higher attainment in class, you will naturally and quickly build up confidence. At the end of your beginners' course, you will then be ready and waiting for a more advanced class, knowing full well that you have already made a good start and have built yourself a rock-hard foundation.

If you are already in a higher class, this book provides a thorough revision so that you can 'brush yourself up' to be ready for more adventure. 'Never jump unless you're sure you can pivot yourself instantly when you land.' By this is meant that foundation work is absolutely essential. Again, the chapter on *Force and Motion* is very useful to you at this stage as you are now gradually and slowly entering the stage of experimentation and research. The more complicated techniques need reasoning. And reasoning needs understanding.

To the teacher

It is a pleasure to present this volume. I hope that on reading it you will feel that it provides a good text book for your class. There is no better way to describe its virtues than to suggest that you read it. And I leave it in your experienced hands.

Note: The 'Art of Fisticuffs' (Chuan Shu 拳術) is also known as 'Chinese Boxing'.

Peter P. Tang

Acknowledgments

I would like to thank my sister who contributed many valuable suggestions and ideas and has made this production possible.

Also, my thanks to my wife for her patience and everlasting co-operation and assistance in the taking of the photographs; and my appreciation to my sons for their enthusiasm and their appearance in the photographs.

Warning

Anyone using this book must have a sincere and responsible mind. There are two ways of doing things – the right way and the wrong way. Only the right way can bring you success. The wisdom and knowledge of this book are both powerful and dangerous. They are to be treated with conscience and respect and NOT to be used 'fooling about'. Accidents must be avoided and when practising with a partner, you must make sure to stop within an inch of the target.

Basic positions

FREQUENTLY, in the course of exercise, there are basic positions which are referred to. Have a good understanding of them and be able to reproduce them accurately. Later, when in doubt, keep referring back to this chapter until you are absolutely sure.

The fist
Notice how the thumb presses against the forefinger and second finger. The fingers should clench solidly, leaving no empty space. The wrist should be straight with the fist. The reason for all these is that on striking a punch home, the impact will not damage the fingers or the wrist.

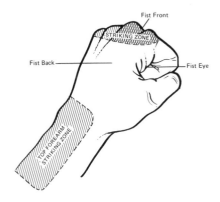

The fist edge

The striking area is the same as that of the edge of hand, i.e., the edge from the base of the little finger to the wrist. A typical target for this blow is the nape of neck at the base of the skull. There the spinal column is at its weakest. The fist edge is typically used in hammer blows when the opponent is in low positions.

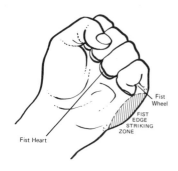

The hand

There are many ways of executing the hand. The style used here is the one illustrated. The four fingers are straight and touching. The thumb should be placed comfortably and naturally with its tip pointing into the hand as shown. This avoids the undesirable protruding of the thumb tip out to the side.

The edge of hand

The striking zone is the edge which extends from the base of the little finger to the wrist. The point of contact is the bony edge of the hand.

The edge of hand is used to execute chops vertically or horizontally. Also, it is used to drive a straight forward strike and is effective as a block against punches and kicks.

Targets are the temple, neck, windpipe, nape of neck, collarbone and solar plexus.

At the moment of contact, it is essential to tense hand and wrist so that they are rigid. Reinforce the blow with the body weight.

The spear hand
The fingers are slightly bent at the knuckle.

Targets should be the more sensitive parts of the body, e.g., testicles, eyes and the abdomenal area. This is because the fingertips are not very strong and cannot deliver very much power.

Tension and rigidity of hand are again the essential features of an effective thrust. The thumb can help by pressing the outside of the index finger.

STRIKING ZONE

The hook
The five finger tips group together to form the hook tip. The wrist bends inward as much as possible.

The hook top is very effective in both blocks and attacks. It is used to block punches and hand strikes with a lifting action.

For attack, it is effective against the lower part of the face, eg. the jaw and the chin.

The hook itself is used to catch an attacking foot. With a lifting action, the opponent can be made to fall.

The hook tip is a strong point for attack. A good target is the eye.

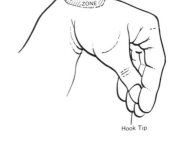

Hook Top

STRIKING ZONE

Hook Tip

The horse stance
This is one of the essential modes of standing. It offers maximum stability while at the same time, movement to any direction can be executed swiftly and effectively. This is attributed to the bending of the knees. The name is derived from its similarity to the position of riding a horse.

The feet are separated by a distance just greater than that of the shoulders. Bend the knees to about 90 degrees. Keep the body straight.

The bow-arrow stance (or bow stance)
This stance is very frequently used
particularly in the case of attack. Not only
does it allow the body to advance, but also
maintains stability. On bringing home a
hard punch, for example, there is a
certain amount of reactive force bouncing
back towards you. This force will be offset
by the bow-arrow stance which maintains
balance. A bent leg and a straight leg give
the name 'Bow-Arrow' which is
frequently simplified into 'Bow Stance'.

The left bow-arrow stance has the left
leg forward and bent.

The right bow-arrow stance has the
right leg forward and bent.

Open the legs with one big step. Bend
the front leg which then supports a
slightly greater share of the body weight.
Keep the other leg straight. Also keep
your waist straight.

The free stance
This is called the 'free stance' because one
leg is free from supporting any weight.
Then, free to do what? Free to be ready
for the next move.

Maintain a position with both legs
bent. Support the body with one leg,
letting the other leg free. At a distance of
half a step, its toes just touch the ground.
Turn the body slightly towards the free
leg.

The left free stance has the left leg free.

The right free stance has the right leg
free.

The L stance

This stance can be regarded as a further development of the bow stance. It differs from the bow stance in that:

i. The bending leg is bent to the maximum so that the body is at its lowest.

ii. The stance is named after the stretched leg, e.g., the left L stance illustrated. This leg is nearly level with the ground similar to the second stroke of the letter L.

The left L stance has the left leg stretched. The right L stance has the right leg stretched.

Most of the body weight is carried by the bent leg. Make sure that both feet lie completely flat on the ground and avoid the heels being lifted.

The ball of the foot

The shaded area is the striking area. The toes must be bent well back. This allows the ball to stand clear, and tightens the muscles which strengthen the striking area. To deliver a powerful kick, the leg is first raised as high as possible with the knee bent. Without stopping and with a strong spring action in the knee, the ball of the foot is sent forward to the target. Targets include the stomach, ribs or chin.

This position is useful when barefooted or wearing soft shoes.

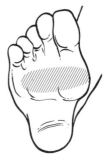

Vulnerable points of the body

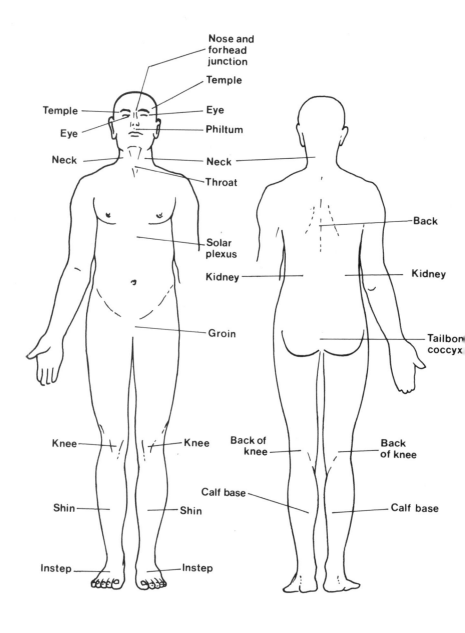

Sequence I

ALL THREE SEQUENCES consist of 32
movements. These movements are so
designed that one leads swiftly to another.
When well practised, each sequence
should be performed from start to finish
in a smooth, continuous and coordinated
manner. Each movement usually consists
of 2 or more actions of arms and legs.
These actions are to be executed
simultaneously, i.e., all at the same time.
However, it may be difficult to do this at
first. So, practise and master the first
action as listed in the instructions. Then
add the second action and so on. A piece of
advice at this point. Do not be impatient
and do not be pushed by the thought that
you are not rushing through the book
quickly enough. These sequences are very
rich sequences which altogether contain
96 skilful techniques. Each technique or
movement is worthy of time and study
and demands perfect mastery. Otherwise,
without perfect mastery, the movements
will become that of a dance. One promise,
and that is once the initial hard work is
over, you will be able to enjoy your speed
and accuracy.

If not enough space is available to you,
for example, if you can only practise in
your small bedroom, do not be
disheartened. Just practise 2 or 3
movements at a time.

Get ready

i. ATTENTION: Put feet together and stand straight. Open hands and hold at the sides. Keep spine straight, chest raised, belly in and spirit high.

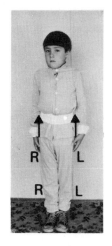

ii. Clench fingers into fists. Raise fists and plant firmly at the sides of waist, fist hearts upwards. With elbows bent, keep arms drawn back.

For the convenience of study, the sequence is divided into 4 parts. (Parts 1 & 2 were demonstrated by William Tang.)

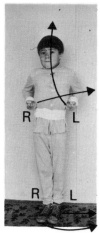

Part 1

1. Block and blow
From previous position:

i. With left foot, move one step to the left, starting a left about turn.

ii. With right foot, advance one more step to complete the about turn of 180° and bend knees to form the horse stance.

SIMULTANEOUSLY:
iii. Raise left arm through the front to above head level to form an UPPER BLOCK against attack to the head. Notice the important position of the fist. The fist has turned so that its wheel now faces upwards. The elbow is bent. The aim of

this block is to force the attacking arm or foot up so as to re-direct its force.

iv. Thrust the right fist straight to the right at the opponent's solar plexus, fist eye upwards. Eyes on right fist.

2. Once again
From previous position:

i. With left foot, advance one step to the right making a right about turn of 180°. Bend knees to keep to the horse stance.

SIMULTANEOUSLY:
ii. Withdraw right arm and push it upward to form an UPPER BLOCK against attack to the head, fist wheel up.

iii. Lower left fist to waist level and thrust straight to the left at the opponent's solar plexus, fist eye up. Eyes on left fist.

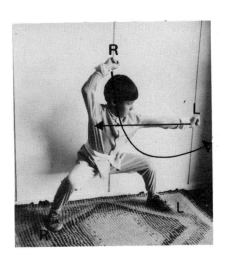

Note: Take note of the characteristics of each technique which are pointed out and discussed. When the same technique reappears later, its characteristics will not be repeatedly discussed again. Only those of new techniques are to be elaborated.

3. Letter K (The position resembles the shape of this letter)
From previous position:

i. Make a left turn and bend left knee to form the LEFT BOW STANCE (see chapter on Basic Positions).

SIMULTANEOUSLY:
ii. Change right fist to the hand. Lower hand to waist level and push forward and upward to effect a PALM-HEEL BLOCK against a direct attack to the face. The effect of the block is to lift the wrist of the attacking arm with your right palm-heel.

iii. Change left fist to the hand, withdraw and hide under right armpit palm down ready for the next action.

4. Don't tell me ('Don't tell me, I don't want to hear.' That is the impression of this position.)
From previous position:

i. Withdraw left foot half a step and shift body weight onto the right leg to form the LEFT FREE STANCE (see chapter on Basic Positions). Note that the right leg is bent and the toes of left foot just touch the ground.

SIMULTANEOUSLY:
ii. Change right hand to fist and return to ready position, i.e., planted at the side of waist, fist heart up.

iii. Raise left hand upward, sweeping across the face to finish up over the left ear and so form a HAND BLOCK against attack to the left ear. Point elbow forwards and keep eyes front.

So far, you have been moving to the left. Now you start to move to the right. Movements 5 to 8 are repetition of 1 to 4 but in the opposite direction.

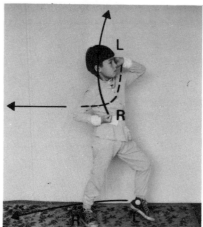

5. Block and blow
From previous position:

i. With a gentle push of the toes of the free left foot, turn left 90° to bring the left foot one step to the left and assume the horse stance.

SIMULTANEOUSLY:
ii. Raise right fist across the front to above head level to form an UPPER BLOCK against attack to the head, fist wheel up, elbow bent.

iii. Change left hand to fist and lower to waist level. In one sweeping motion, thrust fist straight to the left at the opponent's solar plexus, fist eye up. Eyes on left fist.

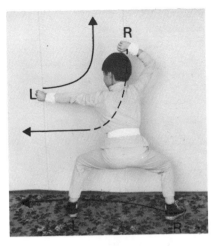

6. Once again
From previous position:

i. With right foot, advance one step to the left making a left about turn of 180° and keep to the horse stance.

SIMULTANEOUSLY:
ii. Withdraw left arm and push it upward to form an UPPER BLOCK against attack to the head, fist wheel up.

iii. Lower right fist to waist level and thrust straight to the right at the opponent's solar plexus, fist eye up. Eyes on right fist.

7. Letter K
From previous position:
i. Make a right body turn and bend right knee to form the RIGHT BOW STANCE.

SIMULTANEOUSLY:
ii. Change left fist to the hand. Lower hand to waist level and push forward and upward to effect a PALM-HEEL BLOCK against a direct attack to the face.

iii. Change right fist to the hand, withdraw and hide under left armpit, palm down ready for the next action.

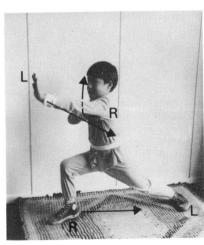

23

8. Don't tell me

From previous position:

i. Withdraw right foot half a step and shift body weight onto the left leg to form the RIGHT FREE STANCE. Note the bending of the left leg and the touching of the ground by the toes of the right free foot.

SIMULTANEOUSLY:
ii. Change left hand to fist and return to ready position.

iii. Raise right hand upward, sweeping across the face to finish up over the right ear and so form a HAND BLOCK against attack to the right ear. Point elbow forwards and keep eyes front.

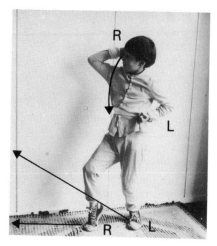

Part 2

9. Spring kick left

a. From previous position:

i. Advance the free right foot one step forward. On landing, keep leg slightly bent to support all the body weight.

ii. Pull left foot up and push the knee forward and as high as you can, keeping a good bend to relax the lower part of the leg.

SIMULTANEOUSLY:
iii. Change right hand to fist and return to ready position.

b. From position a:

i. Spring out the lower left leg sharp and hard to kick the opponent's abdomen with the ball of the foot. To do this, curl the toes well back. This prevents injury to the toes. The kicking leg must be straight and fully extended so as to exert maximum kicking power. Practise this technique accurately and gradually introduce speed so that steps (a) and (b) eventually become one rapid movement. Always keep eyes front.

10. Monkey hook (Resembles the posture of monkeys.)
From previous position:

i. Retreat kicking left foot one big step. Note that the return of a kicking leg is the reverse action of kicking, i.e., bend it first then lower it so that the leg can be recovered quickly and the body's balance maintained. At the same time, left turn 90°. On landing of left foot, bend knee.

ii. Pull right foot near the left foot and maintain balance with toes leaving right heel off the ground. Bend knee to crouch low.

SIMULTANEOUSLY:
iii. Change right fist to hand and describe a semi-circle in the direction of up-left-down ending at the back. By now the hand has developed into a hook, tip up, to hook the attacking foot towards your right leg. Eyes right.

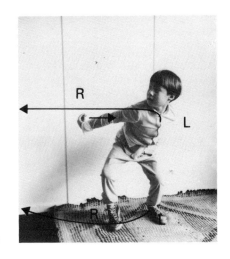

11. No thank you (As if refusing an offer.)
From previous position:

i. Advance left foot one step to the right making a right about turn of 180° and form the horse stance.

SIMULTANEOUSLY:
ii. Change right hook to fist and return to ready position.

iii. Change left fist to hand. With palm facing the opponent, strike directly to his face with the palm heel effecting a PALM HEEL STRIKE. To consolidate the palm heel, you need to tense the five fingers even if the hand shape has to be modified. Eyes on left hand.

12. Middle block

From previous position:

i. Retreat left foot one big step by swinging backwards to make a left about turn of 180° and maintain the horse stance.

SIMULTANEOUSLY:
ii. Change left hand to fist and return to ready position.

iii. Raise right fist to eye level, fist heart towards you and arm bent, and swing elbow outside and inward with the left about turn to effect a MIDDLE OUTSIDE BLOCK against attack to your body (blocking at the outside of the attacking limb). Eyes right. This movement follows closely the previous movement because if your 'No Thank You Palm Heel Strike' is not successful, e.g., being blocked, your opponent will follow up with a blow to your body. Remember to swing your blocking arm around in front of you.

The following movements will move you to the left again.

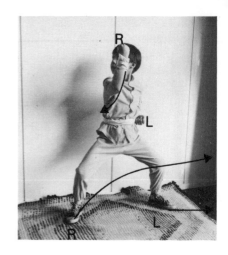

13. Spring kick right

13. Spring kick right (Only the final position is shown here. Refer to Movement 9 for the two detailed steps.) From previous position:

i. Advance left foot one step to the left making a left turn at the same time. On landing, keep leg slightly bent to support all body weight.

ii. Pull right foot up and push knee forward and as high as you can, keeping a good bend to relax the lower leg. Spring out the lower right leg sharp and hard to kick the opponent's abdomen with the ball of the foot, keeping toes curled. Eyes front.

SIMULTANEOUSLY:
iii. Return right fist to ready position.

14. Monkey hook
From previous position:

i. Retreat kicking right foot one big step, (bend leg first then lower it). At the same time turn right and on landing, bend knee.

ii. Pull left foot near the right foot and maintain balance with toes leaving left heel off the ground. Bend knee to crouch low.

SIMULTANEOUSLY:
iii. Change left fist to hand and describe a semi-circle in the direction of up-right-down ending at the back. By now the hand has developed into a hook, tip up, to hook the attacking foot towards your left leg. Eyes left.

15. No thank you
From previous position:

i. Advance right foot one step to the left making a left about turn of 180° and form the horse stance.

SIMULTANEOUSLY:
ii. Change left hook to fist and return to ready position.

iii. Change right fist to hand. With palm facing opponent, strike directly to his face with the palm heel effecting a PALM HEEL STRIKE. Meanwhile, tense the fingers. Eyes on right hand.

16. Middle block
From previous position:

i. Retreat right foot one big step by swinging backwards to make a right about turn and maintain the horse stance.

SIMULTANEOUSLY:
ii. Change right hand to fist and return to ready position.

iii. Raise left fist to eye level, fist heart towards you and arm bent, and swing elbow outside and inward with the right about turn to effect a MIDDLE OUTSIDE BLOCK against attack to your body. Eyes left. Your blocking arm should now be in front of you.

Part 3

(Parts 3 & 4 are demonstrated by Richard W. Tang.)

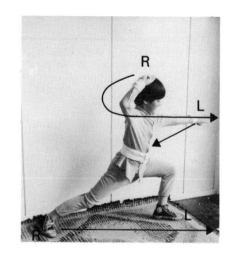

17. Level chop
From previous position:

i. Transform the horse stance into left bow stance by turning your body left, bend left leg and straighten right leg, without lifting the feet.

SIMULTANEOUSLY:
ii. Change right fist to hand and raise to the head, palm up, for protection and in readiness for the next action.

iii. Change left fist to hand and with palm down, start just above right shoulder to sweep horizontally and forcefully to strike at opponent's face, neck or shoulder, effecting a HORIZONTAL EDGE HAND CHOP or LEVEL CHOP. Eyes front. You should take advantage of your body weight, which is transferred to the left leg due to the left bow stance, to strengthen your chop at the moment of impact.

18. Chop again
From previous position:

i. Advance right foot one step forward and bend knee to form the right bow stance.

SIMULTANEOUSLY:
ii. Change left hand to fist and return to ready position.

iii. From the head high position and with palm up, swing right hand in the direction back-side-front horizontally to chop at opponent's head or neck, effecting another horizontal edge hand chop or LEVEL CHOP. Eyes on right hand.

19. Guillotine
From previous position.

i. Without lifting the feet, left turn, bend left leg to support most of the body weight and straighten right leg to form the RIGHT L STANCE (See chapter on Basic Positions). This may be difficult to do at first so give it more practice.

SIMULTANEOUSLY:
ii. Change right hand to fist and with fist heart up, bring fist back to strike straight down the front and effect a GUILLOTINE BLOCK against opponent's advancing kick to your abdomen particularly with his right leg. In this block, 2 striking areas can be used: (1) the striking edge of the fist, i.e., the knuckles especially those of the forefinger and middle finger; (2) the top of the forearm. Eyes right.

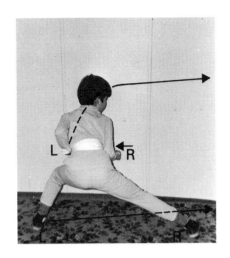

20. Left K punch
From previous position:

i. Advance left foot one step to the right to make a right turn. On landing, keep knee bent to form the left bow stance.

SIMULTANEOUSLY:
ii. Return right fist to ready position.

iii. Punch left fist straight at opponent's face, fist eye up. Eyes front. Relax shoulders with left shoulder slightly forward. To keep the upper half of your body stable, tense the solar plexus.

Now you will start to move back to the right.

21. Level chop

From previous position:

i. Without lifting the feet, make a right about turn. Straighten left leg and bend right leg to form the right bow stance.

SIMULTANEOUSLY:

ii. Change left fist to hand and raise to the head, palm up, for protection and in readiness for the next action.

iii. Change right fist to hand and with palm down, start just above left shoulder to sweep horizontally and forcefully to chop opponent's face, neck or shoulder, effecting a horizontal edge hand chop or LEVEL CHOP. Eyes front.

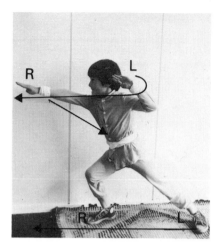

22. Chop again

From previous position:

i. Advance left foot one step forward and bend knee to form the left bow stance.

SIMULTANEOUSLY:

ii. Change right hand to fist and return to ready position.

iii. From the head high position and with palm up, swing left hand in the direction back-side-front horizontally to chop opponent's head or neck, effecting another horizontal edge hand chop or LEVEL CHOP. Eyes on left hand.

23. Guillotine

From previous position:

i. Without lifting the feet, right turn, bend right leg to support most of the body weight and straighten left leg to form the Left L Stance.

SIMULTANEOUSLY:

ii. Change left hand to fist and with fist heart up, bring fist back to strike straight down the front and effect a GUILLOTINE BLOCK against opponent's advancing kick to your abdomen particularly with his left leg. Eyes left. Remember the two striking areas; that of the fist and that of the forearm.

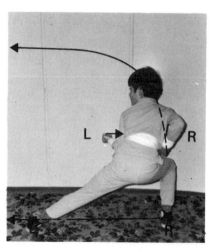

24. Right K punch

From previous position:

i. Advance right foot one step to the left to make a left turn. Keep right knee bent to form the right bow stance.

SIMULTANEOUSLY:
ii. Return left fist to ready position.

iii. Punch right fist straight at opponent's face, fist eye up. Eyes front.

Part 4

25. And side Kick

a. From previous position:

i. Advance left foot as far forward as you can and also making a left turn at the same time. Land to support all body weight.

ii. Pull right foot up to as high as left knee and turn foot inwards so that the heel is jutting outward and edge of foot facing opponent.

SIMULTANEOUSLY:
iii. Return right fist to ready position.

b. From position.

i. Kick right foot with heel or edge of foot straight out to the side to opponent's abdomen or neck. To maintain balance and to empower the kick, twist upper body towards the right, i.e., the kicking leg. Eyes right. Also you should keep body fairly straight. You may find this movement difficult to do at first and keep falling over because of the left leg having to advance. In this case, practise first with both legs in standing position until you can master the kick.

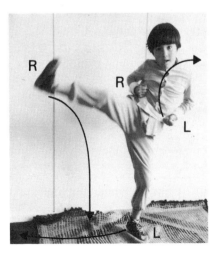

26. Turn to block

From previous position:

i. Drop right foot to the ground.

ii. Pivoting on right toes, make a right about turn to advance left foot one step to the right and form the horse stance.

SIMULTANEOUSLY:

iii. Swing left fist in a large semicircle upwards across the body, first to the right, ending up above left shoulder to block against attack to the body, effecting an INSIDE BLOCK. Eyes on left arm. Fist heart up.

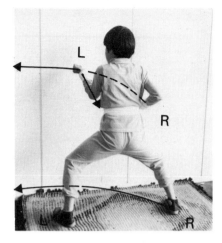

27. Turn to blow

From previous position:

i. Pivoting on left toes, make left about turn to advance right foot one step to the left, maintaining the horse stance.

SIMULTANEOUSLY:

ii. Return left fist to ready position.

iii. Strike right fist sideways to opponent's spleen, fist eye up. Eyes on right fist.

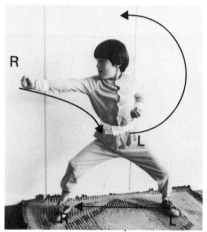

28. Up and down

From previous position:

i. Pull left foot close to right foot and straighten knees.

SIMULTANEOUSLY:

ii. Bend right arm and bring fist, back facing your front, down to block against attack to the right side of your body. Fist heart up.

iii. Swing left fist, elbow bent, from the small of the back, outward and upward in a circular sweep to strike opponent on the side of head, effecting a circular or roundhouse strike, fist eye down. Eyes on left fist.

Now you will move back to the left.

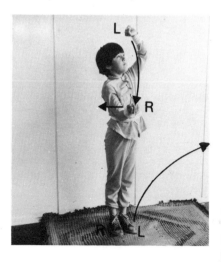

29. And side kick (Only the final
position is shown here. Refer to
movement 25 for details.)
From previous movement:

i. (This movement differs from
movement 25 in that there is no
advancing foot and is therefore easier to
execute.) Pull left foot up to as high as
right knee and turn foot inwards so that
the heel is jutting out and edge of foot
faces opponent. Kick with heel or edge of
foot straight out to the side to opponent's
abdomen or neck. Twist upper body
towards the left slightly. Eyes left.

SIMULTANEOUSLY:
ii. Return both fists to ready position.

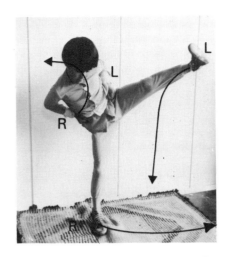

30. Turn to block
From previous position:

i. Drop left foot to the ground.

ii. Pivoting on left toes, make a left about
turn to advance right foot one step to the
left and form the horse stance.

SIMULTANEOUSLY:
iii. Swing right fist in a large semicircle
upwards across the body, first to the left,
ending up above right shoulder to block
against attack to the body, effecting an
inside block, fist heart up. Eyes on right
arm.

31. Turn to blow
From previous position:

i. Pivoting on right toes, make right
about turn to advance left foot one step to
the right, maintaining the horse stance.

SIMULTANEOUSLY:
ii. Return right fist to ready position.

iii. Strike left fist sideways to opponent's
spleen, fist eye up. Eyes on left fist.

32. Up and down

From previous position:

i. Pull right foot close to left foot and straighten knees.

ii. Bend left arm and bring fist, back facing your front, down to block against attack to the left side of your body. Fist heart up.

iii. Swing right fist, elbow bent, from the small of the back, outward and upward in a circular sweep to strike opponent on the side of head, fist eye down, effecting a circular or roundhouse strike. Eyes on right fist.

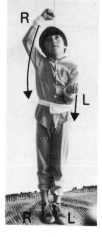

Finish

a. From previous position:

i. Return both fists to ready position.

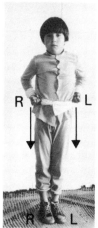

b. From position (a):

i. Change fists to hands.

ii. Lower hands to stand at attention.

34

Sequence 2

THE MOVEMENTS of this sequence
combine more actions of the limbs and leg
movements are heavier. Therefore
complete co-ordination is imperative. To
gain complete co-ordination, you need
patience, determination and extensive
practice. As mentioned in Sequence 1,
each movement is worthy of time and
study. Therefore, practise each action
over and over again until you are
confident that when faced with a real
situation, that action can be applied
without hesitation. To help gain
confidence, a little common sense can go a
long way. Try to understand why an
action is necessary. If you can give a
satisfactory answer to the question
'Why?', confidence will grow quickly.

Get ready
a. ATTENTION: Stand with feet together,
hands open and held at the sides. Keep
spine straight, chest raised, belly in and
spirit high.

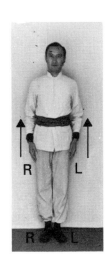

b. READY: Clench fingers into fists. **Raise** fists and plant firmly at the sides of waist, fist hearts up, elbows bent and arms drawn back.

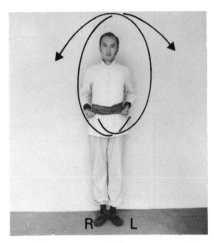

Part 1

1. Butterfly
From ready position:

i. Move left foot one step to the left and form the horse stance.

SIMULTANEOUSLY:
ii. Cross both arms in front of abdomen and swing them right up across the body in a big circle, over the head and down to spread the fists to their sides. Hammer down with force, fist eyes up, effecting double HAMMER BLOWS to strike at opponent on either side in low positions. The striking area is the fist edge, same as the edge of hand. Stop fists at shoulder level. Eyes on left fist. When crossing arms, the striking arm should be inside. In this case the left arm.

2. K punch right

From previous positions:

i. Pivoting on left heel and right toes, left turn to form the left bow stance. Both feet should rest completely on the ground.

SIMULTANEOUSLY:
ii. Return left fist to ready position.

iii. Bend right arm to bring fist back to waist and continue by punching, forcefully, straight forward to effect a K punch, Fist eye up. Eyes front.

3. Letter F

From previous position:

i. Pull right leg up and push the bent knee as high as you can. Then spring out and kick straight forward with ball of foot, effecting a spring kick.

SIMULTANEOUSLY:
ii. Return right fist to ready position.

iii. Thrust left fist straight forward, fist eye up, completing the shape of the letter F. Eyes on left fist.

4. Blow-turn-block

a. From previous position:

i. Drop right foot with a left turn and bend knees to form the horse stance.

SIMULTANEOUSLY:
ii. Return left fist to ready position.

iii. Thrust right fist sideway straight to the right, fist eye up. Eyes on right fist.

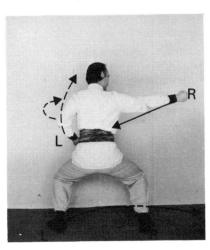

b. From position (*a*):

i. Pivoting on right toes, make a right about turn to advance left foot one step to the right and maintain horse stance.

SIMULTANEOUSLY:
ii. Return right fist to ready position.

iii. Swing the bent left arm with elbow moving in the direction up-out-front in a semicircle, ending with elbow right in front of body, fist heart facing chin, effecting an outside block. Eyes left. Thus, you have completed the 2 step movement of blow-turn-block.

5. Jack in box (What happens when you lift the lid of the box?)
a. From previous position:

i. Stretch and swing left arm up to the left, fist heart outward, to block and deflect blows to the head and shoulder (lifting the lid).

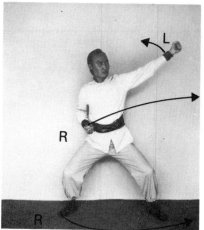

b. From position (*a*):

i. Pivoting on left toes, make a left about turn to advance right foot one step to the left, maintaining horse stance.

SIMULTANEOUSLY:
ii. Thrust right fist straight to the right with force (Jack gives a surprise). Eyes right. The left arm will naturally bend slightly overhead for protection of the head.

6. K hand strike

From previous position:

i. Right turn to advance left foot one step to the right. Bend left leg to form the left bow stance.

SIMULTANEOUSLY:

ii. Return right fist to ready position.

iii. Change left fist to hand. Lower hand to chest level and with the striking edge in front, drive hand straight to target, e.g., opponent's collarbone. Eyes on left hand. Notice how the hand stands in the photograph. This is called the SIDE-STANDING HAND. Remember the striking area of the hand is the edge of the little-finger side of hand (not the little finger) particularly the bony part opposite the knuckle.

7. Strike again

From previous position:

i. Change left hand to fist and return to ready position.

ii. Change right fist to hand and in SIDE-STANDING position, drive straight forward to target. Eyes on right hand. You can help by turning upper body left so that right shoulder moves forward during the strike. Avoid heels leaving the ground.

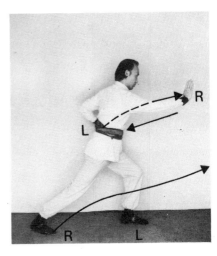

8. F comes back

From previous position:

i. Pull right leg up and push knee to as high as you can, keeping knee bent and foot down. Then spring foot out quickly to kick opponent with ball of foot.

SIMULTANEOUSLY:

ii. Change right hand to fist and return to ready position.

iii. Thrust left fist straight forward, fist eye up. Eyes on left fist. You may lean body slightly forward but not backward, otherwise you will be thrown off your balance. You can let left shoulder move forward.

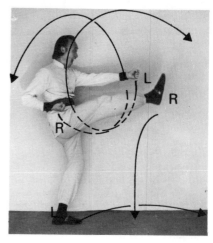

Part 2

(You have been moving all the way to the left. Now you will move back to the right.)

9. Butterfly

From previous position:

i. Let right foot land.

ii. Pivoting on right toes, make a right turn to advance left foot one step. Bend knees to form the horse stance.

SIMULTANEOUSLY:

iii. Cross both arms in front of abdomen, right arm inside, and swing them up across the body in a big circle over the head and continue circular motion to spread fists to their sides. Hammer down with face, fist eyes up, effecting double HAMMER BLOWS. Eyes on right fist.

10. K punch left

From previous position:

i. Pivoting on right heel and left toes, turn right to form the right bow stance. Both feet should rest completely on the ground.

SIMULTANEOUSLY:

ii. Return right fist to ready position.

iii. Bend left arm to bring fist back to waist and continue to punch forcefully straight forward, fist eye up, effecting a K punch. Eyes on left fist.

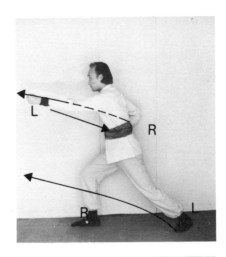

11. Letter F

From previous position:

i. Pull left leg up and push the bent knee as high as you can. Then spring out and kick straight forward with ball of foot, effecting a spring kick.

SIMULTANEOUSLY:

ii. Return left fist to ready position.

iii. Thrust right fist straight forward, fist eye up. Eyes on right fist.

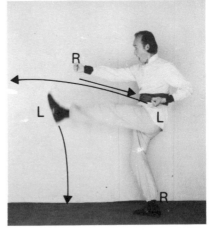

12. Blow-turn-block

a. Drop left foot with a right turn and bend knees to form the horse stance.

SIMULTANEOUSLY:

ii. Return right fist to ready position.

iii. Thrust left fist straight to the left, fist eye up. Eyes on left fist.

b. From position (*a*):

i. Pivoting on left toes, make a left about turn to advance right foot one step to the left and maintain horse stance.

SIMULTANEOUSLY:
ii. Return left fist to ready position.

iii. Swing the bent right arm with elbow moving in the direction up-out-front in a semicircle, ending with elbow right in front of body and fist heart facing chin, effecting an outside block. Eyes right.

13. Jack in box
a. From previous position:

i. Stretch and swing right arm up to the right, fist heart outward, to block and deflect blows to the head and shoulder.

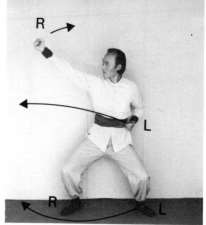

b. From position (*a*):

i. Pivoting on right toes, make a right about turn to advance left foot one step to the right. Maintain horse stance.

SIMULTANEOUSLY:
ii. Thrust left fist straight to the left with force. Eyes left. The right arm will naturally bend slightly overhead for protection.

14. K hand strike

From previous position:

i. Left turn to advance right foot one step to the left. Bend right leg to form right bow stance.

SIMULTANEOUSLY:

ii. Return left fist to ready position.

iii. Change right fist to hand. Lower hand to chest level and with the striking edge in front, drive hand straight to target, e.g., opponent's collarbone. Eyes on right hand.

15. Strike again

From previous position:

i. Change right hand to fist and return to ready position.

ii. Change left fist to hand and in SIDE-STANDING position, drive straight forward to target. Eyes on left hand. You can turn left shoulder forward but avoid heels leaving the ground.

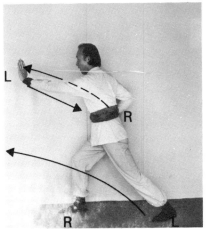

16. F comes back

From previous position:

i. Pull left leg up and push bent knee as high as you can. Then spring out quickly to kick opponent with ball of foot.

SIMULTANEOUSLY:

ii. Change left hand to fist and return to ready position.

iii. Thrust right fist straight forward, fist eye up. Eyes on right fist. You may lean body slightly forward and let right shoulder move forward.

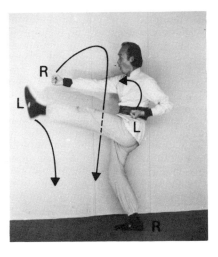

43

Part 3

17. Falling star

From previous position:

i. Let left foot land.

ii. Pivoting on left toes, turn left to advance right foot one step and form the horse stance.

SIMULTANEOUSLY:

iii. Bend right arm to raise fist head high and plunge straight down inside right thigh, effecting the FALLING STAR PLUNGE, fist eye outward.

iv. Change left fist to hand. Raise hand to shoulder level and move across to shield in front of right shoulder. Hand is in standing position with forearm shielding across body. Eyes front.

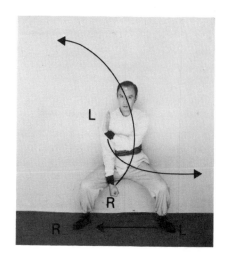

18. Double cross

From previous position:

i. Bring left foot close to right foot and stand straight.

SIMULTANEOUSLY:

ii. Swing right arm in a big circular motion across body, first to left, then up to right to effect an upper block, fist heart outward.

iii. Change left hand to fist and swing downward to lower left, fist crossing inside the up rising right arm, to effect a lower parry, fist heart inward, thus completing the cross with a double blocking action. Eyes front.

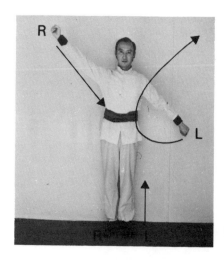

19. Jumping jack (This time Jack jumps at him as well!)

a. From previous position:

i. Lift left leg, keeping knee bent and foot down.

SIMULTANEOUSLY:

ii. Return right fist to ready position.

iii. Swing left arm up in a semicircle to execute an upper block, fist heart front. Eyes left.

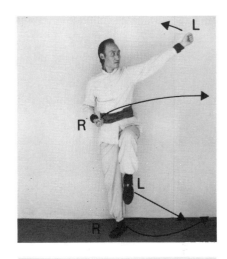

b. From position (*a*):

i. With a push from right foot, jump to advance left foot one step to the left, making a left about turn at the same time. It is important to note that the jump is not intended to gain height but to GAIN DISTANCE. So avoid body bobbing up and down.

ii. As soon as left foot lands, pivot on left toes to complete the about turn and advance the right foot. Bend knees to form the horse stance.

SIMULTANEOUSLY:

iii. Thrust right fist straight out to the right, fist eye up. Eyes right. Left arm will automatically bend overhead.

20. Hook a pair

a. From previous position:

i. Change left fist to hook and hook downwards pass left knee to the back, hooking off an attack to the left e.g., a kick. This hook, when successful, can continue to lift attacker's foot throwing him off balance.

b. From position (*a*):

i. Change right fist to hook and with upper body turning left, send hook to left knee, hook tip down. Eyes left.

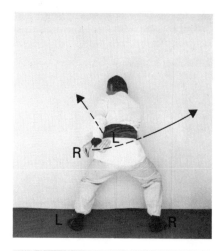

c. From position (*b*):

i. Continue right hook towards the right, hooking off further attack and throwing opponent off balance when applicable. On completion, change hook to fist, and hold at shoulder level, fist eye up. Eyes right.

ii. Change left hook to fist, and forward to middle blocking position, (see photograph), fist heart up.

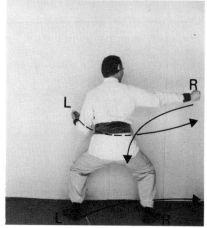

21. K hand strike

From previous position:

i. Pivoting on right toes, turn right to advance left foot one step to the right. Bend left knee to form the left bow stance.

SIMULTANEOUSLY:

ii. Move right arm to the back and bend wrist, fist heart up ready for the next dynamic action. Also it acts as a lower parry.

iii. Change left fist to hand, and in side standing position, drive forward to strike opponent with the striking edge. This time, vary the striking path as a slightly curved path upwards. Note that when this movement is executed immediately after the last movement, the left hook of the

last movement is not changed to fist
but to hand directly. Eyes on left hand.

22. Humpty Dump
From previous position:

i. Advance right foot one step forward
and form the right bow stance.

SIMULTANEOUSLY:
ii. Swing right fist in one big circular
motion from back to above head and
hammer down as if to break opponent
into pieces. Note the fist heart is up and
that you meet the back of the hammering
fist with the left hand. Eyes front.

23. Stop the heart
From previous position:

i. Advance left foot one step forward and
form the left bow stance.

SIMULTANEOUSLY:
ii. Read this carefully. From the position
of left hand holding right fist of last
movement, change left hand to fist, turn
clockwise so that fist heart is down.
Change right fist to hand and hold left fist
with fingers over back of fist, so that
palm-heel is pushing against fist-front.
This combination enables the force from
the right arm to be transmitted
completely to the left elbow. Bring the
combined hand-fist first to near the right
armpit. Then push forcefully to the left,

ejecting the left elbow to strike at the heart of opponent, effecting a REINFORCED ELBOW STRIKE. Eyes on left elbow.

24. Hit the sky
From previous position:

i. Bring right foot close to left foot, turning right at the same time and stand straight.

SIMULTANEOUSLY:
ii. Strike left fist up to overhead position.

iii. Change right hand to fist and swing towards the right to middle blocking position. Eyes front.

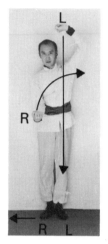

Part 4
(Move to right.)

25. Falling star
From previous position:

i. Move right foot one step to the right and form the horse stance.

SIMULTANEOUSLY:
ii. Plunge left fist straight down inside left thigh, effecting the falling star plunge, fist eye outward.

iii. Change right fist to hand. Raise hand to shoulder level and move across to shield in front of left shoulder, with hand in standing position and forearm shielding across body. Eyes front.

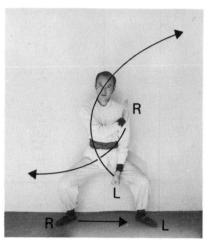

26. Double cross

From previous position:

i. Bring right foot close to left foot and stand straight.

SIMULTANEOUSLY:

ii. Swing left arm in a big circular motion across body, first to right, then up to left to effect an upper block, fist heart outward.

iii. Change right hand to fist and swing downward to lower right, crossing the inside of the up rising left arm, to effect a lower parry, fist heart inward. Eyes front.

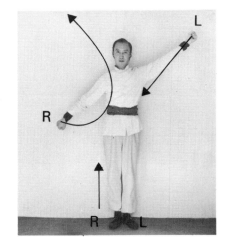

27. Jumping Jack

a. From previous position:

i. Lift right leg, keeping knee bent and foot down.

SIMULTANEOUSLY:

ii. Return left fist to ready position.

iii. Swing right arm up in a semicircle to execute an upper block, fist heart front. Eyes right.

b. From position (*a*):

i. With a push from left foot, jump to advance right foot one step to the right, starting a right about turn at the same time. Avoid body bobbing up and down.

ii. As soon as right foot has landed, pivot on right toes to complete the about turn and advance the left foot. Form the horse stance.

SIMULTANEOUSLY:

iii. Thrust left fist straight out to the left, fist eye up. Eyes left. Right arm will automatically bend overhead.

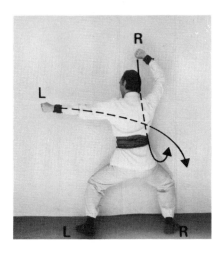

28. Hook a pair

a. From previous position:

i. Change right fist to hook and hook downwards pass right knee to the back, hooking off an attack to the right, e.g., a kick.

ii. Change left fist to hook and with upper body turning right, send hook to right knee, hook tip down. Eyes right.

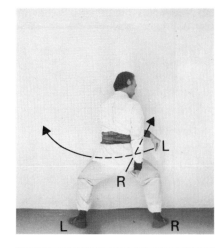

b. From position (*a*):

i. Continue left hook towards the left, hooking off further attack. On completion, change hook to fist, hold at shoulder level, fist eye up. Eyes left.

ii. Change right hook to fist and move forward to middle blocking position, fist heart up.

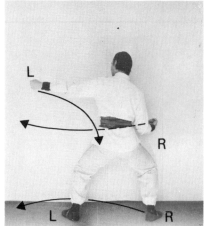

29. K hand strike

From previous position:

i. Pivoting on left toes, turn left to advance right foot one step to left. Form the right bow stance.

SIMULTANEOUSLY:
ii. Swing left arm to the back, wrist bent, fist heart up, to effect a lower parry.

iii. Change right fist to hand, and in side standing position, drive forward in a slightly curved, upward path to strike opponent with the striking edge. Eyes on right hand.

30. Humpty Dump

From previous position:

i. Advance left foot one step forward and form the left bow stance.

SIMULTANEOUSLY:

ii. Swing left fist in one big circular motion from back to above head and hammer down, fist heart up. Meet the back of the hammering fist with the right hand. Eyes front.

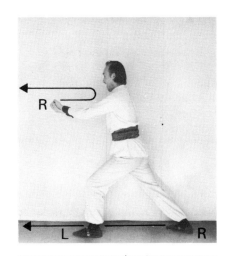

31. Stop the heart

From previous position:

i. Advance right foot one step forward and form the right bow stance.

SIMULTANEOUSLY:

ii. Change right hand to fist, turn anti-clockwise so that fist heart is down. Change left fist to hand to hold right fist with palm-heel pushing against fist-front. Bring this combined hand-fist near to left armpit. Then push forcefully to the right, ejecting the right elbow to strike at opponent's heart, effecting a reinforced elbow strike. Eyes on right elbow.

32. Hit the sky

From previous position:

i. Bring left foot close to right foot, turning left at the same time and stand straight.

SIMULTANEOUSLY:

ii. Strike right fist up to overhead position.

iii. Change left hand to fist and swing to the left to middle blocking position. Eyes front.

Finish

a. From previous position:

i. Return both fists to ready position.

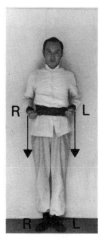

b. From position (*a*):

i. Change both fists to hands. Lower hands and stand at attention.

Sequence 3

Get ready

a. ATTENTION: Stand with feet together, hands open and held at the sides. Keep spine straight, chest raised, belly in and spirit high.

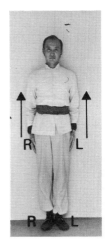

b. READY: Clench fingers into fists. Raise fists and plant firmly at the sides of waist, fist hearts up, elbows bent and arms drawn back.

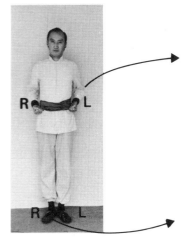

Part 1

(Move to left.)

1. K hand strike

From previous position:

i. Pivoting on left heel and right toes, make a left turn.

ii. Advance right foot one step forward and form the right bow stance.

SIMULTANEOUSLY:
iii. Change left fist to hand and in side-standing position, drive straight forward to target. Eyes on left hand. Help by turning upper body right so that left shoulder moves forward during the strike. Avoid heels leaving the ground.

2. Double chop

a. From previous position:

i. Without lifting the feet, make a left about turn. Straighten right leg and bend left knee to form the left bow stance.

SIMULTANEOUSLY:
ii. Straighten left wrist so that palm is down. Swing hand all the way horizontally with the about turn to chop opponent with the edge of hand, effecting a level chop or horizontal edge hand chop. Eyes on left hand.

b. From position (*a*):

i. Change left hand to fist and return to ready position.

ii. Change right fist to hand and with palm up, swing hand back-side-front horizontally to chop again at opponent. Eyes on right hand.

3. Eagle's wings

a. From previous position:

i. Change left fist to hand and with palm up, thrust swiftly over and along right hand to spear at opponent with fingertips effecting a SPEAR HAND THRUST. The hand is held slightly cupped with fingers bent slightly at the first knuckles. This is not a powerful blow as compared to a punch or a chop because the fingertips are not particularly strong. Therefore, the more sensitive parts of opponent's body should be aimed, e.g., testicles, eyes and the abdomenal area. There are many occasions at close-quarters when this form of attack can be employed. Eyes on left hand.

ii. Bring right hand back and keep in front of chest, palm down.

b. From position (*a*):

i. Without lifting feet, make a right about turn. Straighten left leg and bend right knee to form the right bow stance.

SIMULTANEOUSLY:

ii. Change spear hand to hook and turn clockwise so that hook tip is down. This returns the fingers to a safe position and also the wrist at the top can be used to block and protect.

iii. Drive right hand, in side-standing position, forward to strike with edge of hand, thus completing the spreading of the eagle's wings. Eyes on right hand.

4. Double block

From previous position:

i. Pivoting on right toes, turn right to advance left foot half a step. On landing, only touch ground with toes leaving most of body weight to the right leg, forming the left free stance.

SIMULTANEOUSLY:
ii. Change right hand to fist and swing in circular motion outward and upward to above head level and effect an upper block. Fist heart front.

iii. Change left hook to fist and swing up-front-down ending on left knee, fist heart backward, effecting a low parry. Eyes left.

These two arm actions, together with a slight twist of the body, actually help the right turn and the formation of the left free stance.

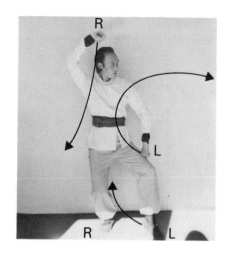

5. Guillotine

5. Guillotine (This movement differs from the Guillotine Movement of Sequence 1 in many ways. (i) There is an additional step (a) which delivers an inverted-fist strike. (ii) The guillotine block takes place over a horse stance.)

a. From previous position:

i. Lift left leg, keeping knee bent and foot down while straightening right leg.

SIMULTANEOUSLY:
ii. Drop right fist to the back to effect a block.

iii. Swing left fist up and to the left to effect an inverted-fist strike, fist heart up. Eyes on left fist.

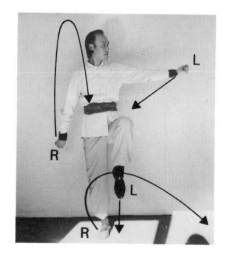

b. From position (*a*):

i. Jump with a push from the right leg to make a left about turn at the same time.

ii. Land left foot first naturally.

iii. Land right foot and form the horse stance.

SIMULTANEOUSLY:
iv. Return left fist to ready position.

v. Swing right fist from back up to overhead. Then bend elbow and with fist heart up, press forearm straight down the front to effect a guillotine block. Eyes on right fist.

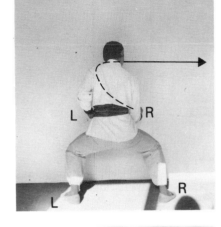

6. Elbow strike

a. From previous position:

i. Pivoting on left toes and right heel, turn right and form the right bow stance

SIMULTANEOUSLY:
ii. Change right fist to hand and with palm down, first move over to just above left shoulder, then sweep across horizontally to effect a level chop. Eyes on right hand.

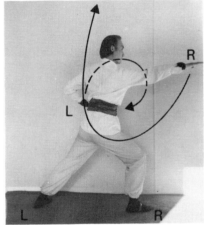

b. From position (*a*):

i. Turn right hand clockwise so that palm is up. Sweep the hand through a big circle front-down-back and up to above head level, effecting a sweeping hand block. Then bend elbow with palm front.

ii. Swing left elbow and strike from the outside inwards to opponent's upper regions, e.g., face. This can be helped with a spring in the hips. Eyes front. This is a very powerful strike, but its range is limited. Therefore it can be most effective at close distance. Targets include the chin, stomach and abdomen.

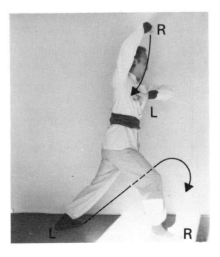

7. Peacock's tail

a. From previous position:

i. Pivoting on right foot, turn right and pull left leg up and hold with knee bent and toes pointing down.

SIMULTANEOUSLY:

ii. Change right hand to fist and drop to meet left fist at chest level, fist front to fist front, both fist hearts down, arms level and elbows out. Eyes left.

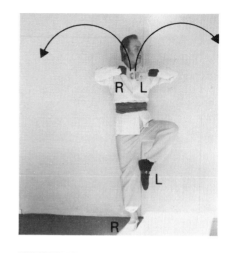

b. From position (*a*):

i. Snap both fists up and out to the sides to strike powerfully with both inverted fists, effecting a double inverted-fist strike like the opening up of the peacock's tail. Eyes on left fist. Keep both arms slightly bent and stand firm on the single right leg.

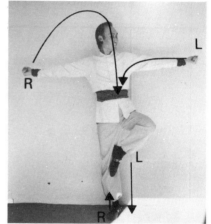

8. All fall down

a. From previous position:

i. Turn left to land left foot and keep knee slightly bent.

ii. Lift right foot slightly off the ground.

SIMULTANEOUSLY:

iii. Change left fist to hand and bring the hand back to the front to press downwards, palm down.

iv. Change right fist to hand and raise up and to the front to press downwards together with the left hand. Eyes front.

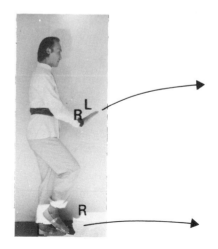

b. From position (*a*):

i. Advance right foot one step forward and form the right bow stance.

SIMULTANEOUSLY:
ii. First bend the elbows. Then straighten the arms and push forward with both hands so that 'all fall down'. Eyes on hands.

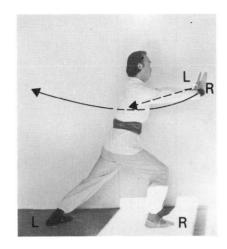

Part 2

(Move to right.)

9. K hand strike
From previous position:

i. Without lifting feet, make a left about turn and form the left bow stance.

SIMULTANEOUSLY:
ii. Change left hand to fist and return to ready position.

iii. Bring right hand back and in side-standing position, drive straight forward to strike target with edge of hand. Eyes on right hand. Help by turning upper body left so that right shoulder moves forward during the strike. Avoid heels leaving ground.

10. Double chop

a. From previous position:

i. Without lifting the feet, make a right about turn and form the right bow stance.

SIMULTANEOUSLY:
ii. Straighten right wrist so that palm is down. Swing hand all the way horizontally with the about turn to chop opponent with the edge of hand, effecting a level chop. Eyes on right hand.

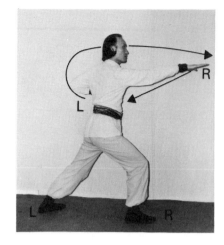

b. From position (*a*):

i. Change right hand to fist and return to ready position.

ii. Change left fist to hand and with palm up, swing hand back-side-front horizontally to chop again at opponent. Eyes on left hand.

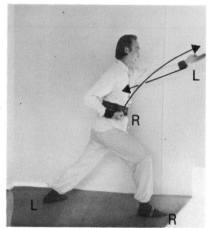

11. Eagle's wings

a. From previous position:

i. Change right fist to hand and with palm up, thrust swiftly over and along left hand to spear at opponent with fingertips, effecting a SPEAR HAND THRUST. Eyes on right hand.

ii. Bring left hand back and keep in front of chest palm down.

b. From position (*a*):

i. Without lifting feet, make a left about turn and form the left bow stance.

SIMULTANEOUSLY:
ii. Change spear hand to hook and turn anti-clockwise so that hook tip is down.

iii. Drive left hand, in side-standing position, forward to strike with edge of hand, completing the spreading of the eagle's wings. Eyes on left hand.

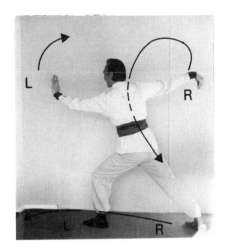

12. Double block
From previous position:

i. Pivoting on left toes, turn left to advance right foot half a step. On landing, only touch ground with toes forming the right free stance.

SIMULTANEOUSLY:
ii. Change left hand to fist and swing in circular motion outward and upward to above head level and effect an upper block. Fist heart front.

iii. Change right hook to fist and swing up-front-down ending on right knee, fist heart backward, effecting a low parry. Eyes right.

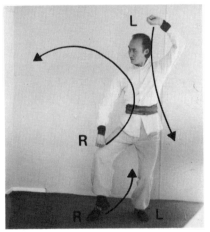

These two arm actions, together with a slight twist of the body, actually help the left turn and the formation of the right free stance.

13. Guillotine

a. From previous position:

i. Lift right leg, keeping knee bent and foot down while straightening left leg.

SIMULTANEOUSLY:
ii. Drop left fist to the back to effect a block.

iii. Swing right fist up and to the right to effect an inverted-fist strike, fist heart up. Eyes on right fist.

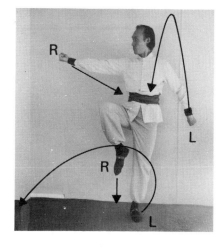

b. From position (*a*):

i. Jump with a push from the left leg to make a right about turn at the same time.

ii. Land right foot first naturally.

iii. Land left foot and form the horse stance.

SIMULTANEOUSLY:
iv. Return right fist to ready position.
v. Swing left fist from behind up to overhead. Then bend elbow and with fist heart up, press forearm straight down the front to effect a guillotine block. Eyes on left fist.

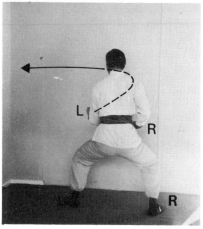

14. Elbow strike

a. From previous position.

i. Pivoting on right toes and left heel, turn left and form the left bow stance.

SIMULTANEOUSLY:
ii. Change left fist to hand and with palm down, first move over to just above right shoulder, then sweep across horizontally to effect a level chop. Eyes on left hand.

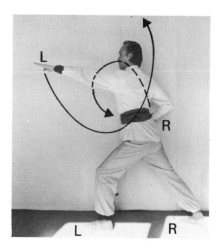

b. From position (*a*):

i. Turn left hand anti-clockwise so that palm is up. Sweep the hand through a big circle front-down-back and up to above head level, effecting a sweeping hand block. Then bend elbow with palm front.

ii. Swing right elbow and strike from the outside inwards to opponent's upper region. Spring the hips to help. Eyes front.

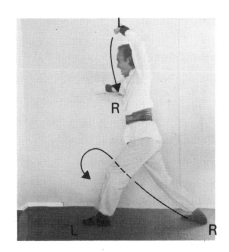

15. Peacock's tail
a. From previous position:

i. Pivoting on left foot, turn left and pull right leg up. Hold with knee bent and toes pointing down.

SIMULTANEOUSLY:
ii. Change left hand to fist and drop to meet right fist at chest level, fist front to fist front and both fist hearts down, arms level and elbows out. Eyes right.

b. From position (*a*):

i. Snap both fists up and out to the sides to strike powerfully with both inverted fists. Eyes on right fist. Keep both arms slightly bent and stand firm.

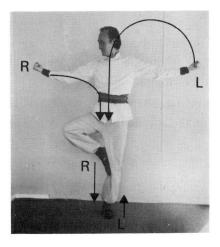

16. All fall down

a. From previous position:

i. Turn right to land right foot and keep knee slightly bent.

ii. Lift left foot slightly off the ground.

SIMULTANEOUSLY:
iii. Change right fist to hand and bring the hand back to the front to press downwards, palm down.

iv. Change left fist to hand, raise up and to the front to press downwards together with the right hand. Eyes front.

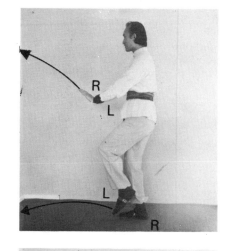

b. From position (*a*):

i. Advance left foot one step forward and form the left bow stance.

SIMULTANEOUSLY:
ii. First bend the elbows. Then straighten the arms and push forward with both hands so that 'all fall down'. Eyes on hands.

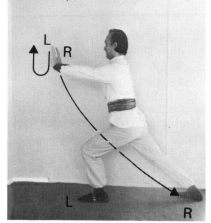

Part 3

(Move to left.)

17. Tick to Break (How do you tick? Answer: '✓')

a. From previous position: (Down stroke of the tick)

i. Pivoting on left heel, turn upper body right. Bend left leg completely so that the hips are as close to the lower leg as possible and the already straight right leg lies as flat as possible over the ground, thus forming the right L stance.

SIMULTANEOUSLY:
ii. Change left hand to hook. Hook

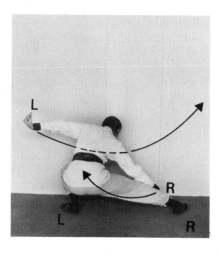

clockwise and hold with hook tip up, arm raised.

iii. Sweep right hand downwards and across to reach the right foot with upper body also leaning towards the right, providing a good blocking and parrying effect. Eyes on right hand.

b. (Upward and breaking stroke of the tick) From position (*a*):

i. Straighten left leg and bend right leg to form the right bow stance. The effect of this is that the upper body is pushed forward to the right and has also turned right. The transformation from the L stance to the bow stance requires strong legs and may be difficult at first. So give it plenty of practice.

SIMULTANEOUSLY:
ii. Change right hand to hook and hook to the back, hook tip up.

iii. Change left hook to fist and in one sweeping motion from back to front, send fist forward to strike opponent's middle or lower region, e.g., solar plexus, kidney or groin. This is a hook punch in which the arm is slightly bent and the fist is inverted, ie, fist heart is up. The punch is delivered like the action of a hook. Eyes on left fist.

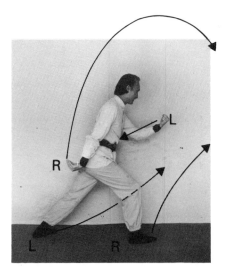

18. Flying kick

From previous position:

i. Lift left foot and be ready for the jump.

ii. With a great push from the right leg, jump as high as you can. (i) and (ii) together make a good jump because one helps the other. Therefore the two actions must be completely coordinated. At the peak of the jump, kick right foot flying out to attack with the ball of the foot, e.g., to opponent's face or neck.

SIMULTANEOUSLY:
iii. Return left fist to ready position.

iv. Change right hook to hand and swing up and front in a semicircular motion to clap the back of the flying foot. The clap should be accurate, loud and clear and should be completed before the left foot lands. Eyes on right foot.

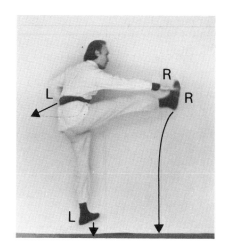

19. Pendulum

a. From previous position:

i. Land left foot gently on the tips of toes.

ii. Land right foot gently in front of left foot and keep knee bent.

SIMULTANEOUSLY:
iii. Straighten left arm and move fist to the back with fist heart up. Eyes front.

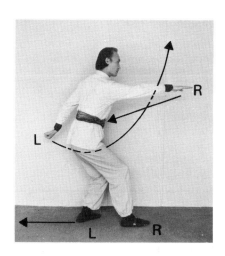

b. From position (*a*):

i. Move left foot half a step backward to perfect the right bow stance.

SIMULTANEOUSLY:
ii. Change right hand to fist and return to ready position.

iii. Swing the straight left arm from back to upper front like a pendulum, led by the striking areas, namely the knuckle edge of the fist and the top forearm, effecting the pendulum strike. Eyes on left fist.

20. Windmill drop

a. From previous position:

i. Pivoting on right heel, turn left and bring left foot back half a step to form the left free stance.

SIMULTANEOUSLY:
ii. Continue the swinging pendulum movement of the left arm from above head down to the left, fist heart up. Eyes on left fist.

iii. Straighten right arm and join the rotational movement, now from lower right to upper right, fist wheel front. The windmill is now well in action. Do not tense the shoulders.

b. From position (*a*):

i. Pivoting on the toes of both feet, turn left so that the legs are crossed with the left in front. Bend knees completely to crouch low.

SIMULTANEOUSLY:
ii. Continue rotational movement of left arm down the left side and up the back, keeping fist heart up.

iii. Like the vanes of a windmill, the right arm sends its fist down the right side with its striking area leading and fist heart up, executing a powerful windmill drop. Eyes on right fist.

This movement is not made for show. It has both offensive and defensive values.

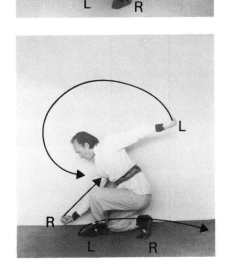

21. Side kick left

a. From previous position:

i. Straighten legs to stand up while pivoting on toes of both feet, make a right about turn. Advance left foot one step to form the left bow stance with upper body turned slightly right.

SIMULTANEOUSLY:
ii. Continue circular movement of left arm up, overhead and to the front to cross with right arm over the right wrist. Change both fists to hands. Eyes on hands.

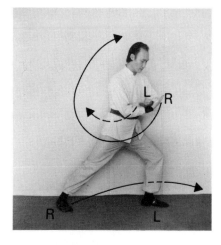

b. From position (*a*):

i. With a push from right foot, advance right foot, across the back of left foot, one step to the left.

SIMULTANEOUSLY:
ii. Change left hand to hook and hook to the back, hook tip up.

iii. Sweep right hand to the right and up to block overhead, palm front. Eyes left.

c. From position (*b*):

i. Raise left leg, knee bent, then spring out to the left to kick with heel or edge of foot forcefully. Eyes left.

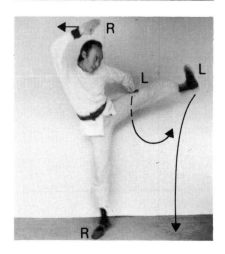

22. Roundhouse punch

a. From previous position:

i. Land left foot.

SIMULTANEOUSLY:

ii. Change right hand to fist and move slightly to the back.

iii. Change left hook to fist, and move to the front with fist eye right. Eyes left.

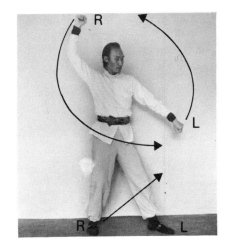

b. From position (*a*):

i. Pivoting on left foot, turn left and lift right foot with knee bent.

SIMULTANEOUSLY:

ii. Swing left fist to upper left.

iii. In a roundhouse or circular motion, swing right fist down and to the outside of right knee. Eyes on right fist.

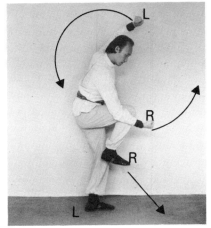

c. From position (*b*):

i. Land right foot in front of left foot but only to touch ground with the toes. With left leg bent, form the right free stance.

SIMULTANEOUSLY:

ii. Continue circular motion with left fist down the back to the ready position. The left fist has now described one complete circle.

iii. Continue the roundhouse movement of the right fist to punch to the front in an upward manner, fist eye to the left exposing the deadly striking zone. The arm can be slightly bent. Eyes on right fist.

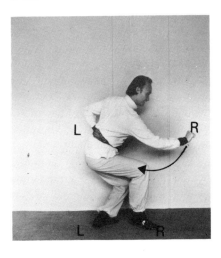

23. Elbow strike

a. From previous position:

i. Push body up and bring right fist to inside of right knee.

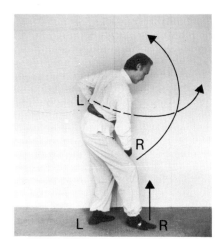

b. From position (*a*):

i. Straighten left leg and raise right leg with knee bent.

SIMULTANEOUSLY:
ii. Raise both arms, with left fist now changed to hand, to start a circular blocking motion. Eyes on right fist.

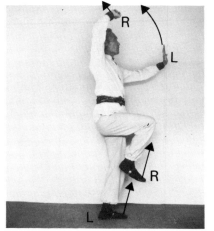

c. From position (*b*):

i. With a push from left foot, jump.

SIMULTANEOUSLY:
ii. Continue upward circular motion of both arms to above head.

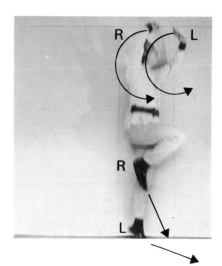

d. From position (*c*):

i. Land right foot first. Bend knee slightly to support body weight.

ii. Land left foot to the left on toes.

SIMULTANEOUSLY:
iii. Complete circular motion of arms to the right, ending over right chest, elbows bent. Change left hand to fist. Also change right fist to hand to cover left fist, palm against fist front. Eyes slightly to right.

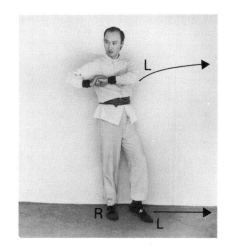

e. From position (*d*):

i. Advance left foot one step to the left and form the left bow stance.

SIMULTANEOUSLY:
ii. Push the hand-fist combination to the left, shooting out the left elbow with the combined force of both arms and at shoulder level. Eyes front.

24. Clap the foot
a. From previous position:

i. Pivoting on toes of both feet, make a right about turn.

SIMULTANEOUSLY:
ii. Move arms up to split the hand-fist combination. Change left fist to hand and swing to the front, palm up.

iii. Swing right hand to the back, palm down. Eyes front.

b. From position (*a*):

i. Straighten left leg and kick to the front, keeping foot straight with leg.

SIMULTANEOUSLY:
ii. Change left hand to fist and return to ready position.

iii. Swing right hand up and to the front to clap left foot accurately, loud and clear. Eyes front.

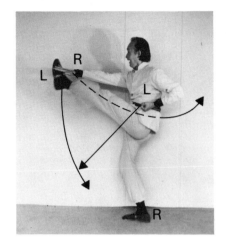

Part 4

(Move to right.)

25. Tick to break
a. From previous position:

i. Land left foot in front of right foot. Turn upper body right. Bend right leg completely while sliding left foot further to the left keeping left leg straight, thus forming the left L stance.

SIMULTANEOUSLY:
ii. Change right hand to hook. Hook to the back and hold with tip up, arm raised.

iii. Change left fist to hand to reach the left foot with upper body also leaning towards the left. Eyes on left hand.

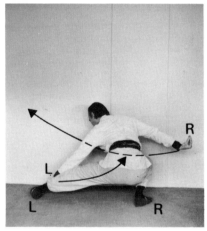

b. From position (*a*):

i. Straighten right leg and bend left leg to form the left bow stance, so that upper body is pushed forward to the left and has also turned left.

SIMULTANEOUSLY:
ii. Change left hand to hook and hook to the back, tip up.

iii. Change right hook to fist and in one sweeping motion from back to front, send fist forward to strike opponent's middle or lower region. This is a hook punch in which the arm is slightly bent and fist inverted. Eyes on right fist.

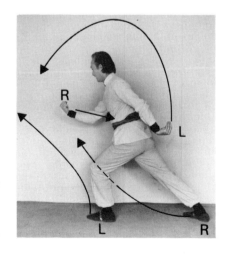

26. Flying kick

From previous position:

i. Lift right foot and ready for the jump.

ii. With a great push from the left leg, jump as high as you can. At the peak of the jump, kick left foot flying out to attack with the ball of the foot.

SIMULTANEOUSLY:

iii. Return right fist to ready position.

iv. Change left hook to hand and swing up and front in a semicircular motion to clap the back of the flying foot accurately, loud and clear. Eyes on left foot.

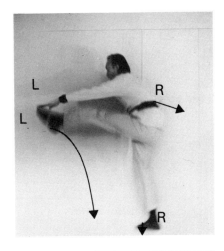

27. Pendulum

a. From previous position:

i. Land right foot gently on the tips of toes.

ii. Land left foot gently in front of right foot and keep knee bent.

SIMULTANEOUSLY:

iii. Straighten right arm and move fist to the back with fist heart up. Eyes front.

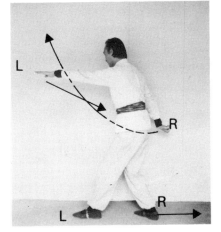

From position (*a*):

i. Move right foot half a step backward to perfect the left bow stance.

SIMULTANEOUSLY:

ii. Change left hand to fist and return to ready position.

iii. Swing the straight right arm from back to upper front like the pendulum, led by the striking areas. Eyes on right fist.

28. Windmill drop

a. From previous position:

i. Pivoting on left heel, turn right and bring right foot back half a step to form the right free stance.

SIMULTANEOUSLY:

ii. Continue the pendulum movement of the right arm from above head down to the right, fist heart up. Eyes on right fist.

iii. Straighten left arm and join the rotational movement, now from lower left to upper left, fist wheel front. The windmill is now well in action. Do not tense the shoulders.

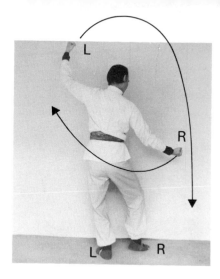

b. From position (*a*):

i. Pivoting on the toes of both feet, turn right so that the legs are crossed with the right in front. Bend knees completely to crouch low.

SIMULTANEOUSLY:

ii. Continue rotational movement of right arm down the right side and up the back, fist heart up.

iii. Like the vanes of a windmill, the left arm sends its fist down the left side with its striking area leading and fist heart up, executing a powerful windmill drop. Eyes on left fist.

29. Side kick right

a. From previous position:

i. Straighten legs to stand up while pivoting on toes of both feet, make a left about turn. Advance right foot one step to form the right bow stance with upper body turned slightly left.

SIMULTANEOUSLY:

ii. Change both fists to hands. Continue circular movement of right arm up, overhead and to the front to cross with left arm over left wrist. Eyes on hands.

b. From position (*a*):

i. With a push from left foot, advance left foot, across the back of right foot, one step to the right.

SIMULTANEOUSLY:
ii. Change right hand to hook and hook to the back, tip up.

iii. Sweep left hand to the left and up to block overhead, palm front. Eyes right.

c. From position (*b*):

i. Raise right leg, knee bent, then spring out to the right to kick with heel or edge of foot forcefully. Eyes right.

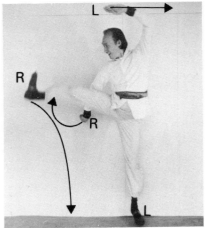

30. Roundhouse punch
a. From previous position:

i. Land right foot.

SIMULTANEOUSLY:
ii. Change left hand to fist and move slightly to the back.

iii. Change right hook to fist, and move to the front with fist eye left. Eyes right.

b. From position (*a*):

i. Pivoting on right foot, turn right and lift left foot with knee bent.

SIMULTANEOUSLY:
ii. Swing right fist to upper right.

iii. In a roundhouse movement, swing left fist down and to the outside of left knee. Eyes on left fist.

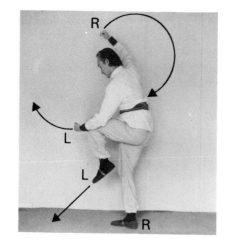

c. From position (*b*):

i. Land left foot in front of right foot but only to touch ground with toes. With right leg bent, form the left free stance.

SIMULTANEOUSLY:
ii. Continue circular motion with right fist down the back to the ready position. The right fist has now described one complete circle.

iii. Continue the roundhouse movement of the left fist to punch to the front in an upward manner, fist eye to the right. The arm can be slightly bent. Eyes on left fist.

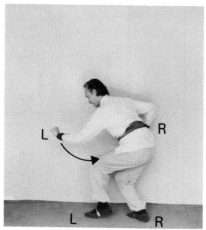

31. Elbow strike

a. From previous position:

i. Push body up and bring left fist to inside of left knee.

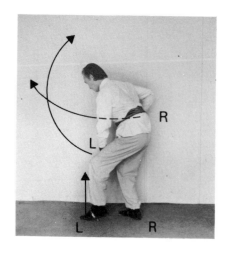

b. From position (*a*):

i. Straighten right leg and raise left leg with knee bent.

SIMULTANEOUSLY:

ii. Raise both arms, with right fist now changed to hand, to start a circular blocking motion. Eyes on left fist.

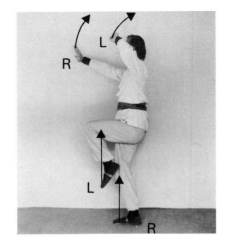

c. From position (*b*):

i. With a push from right foot, jump.

SIMULTANEOUSLY:

ii. Continue upward circular motion of both arms to above head.

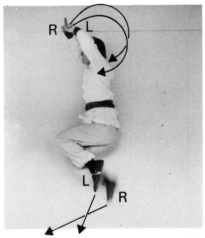

d. From position (*c*):

i. Land left foot first. Bend knee slightly to support body weight.

ii. Land right foot to the right with toes.

SIMULTANEOUSLY:

iii. Complete circular motion of arms to the left, ending over left chest, elbows bent. Change right hand to fist. Also change left fist to hand to cover right fist, palm against fist front. Eyes slightly to left.

e. From position (*d*):

i. Advance right foot one step to the right and form the right bow stance.

SIMULTANEOUSLY:
ii. Push the hand-fist combination to the right, shooting out the right elbow with the combined force of both arms and at shoulder level. Eyes front.

32. Clap the foot

a. From previous position:

i. Pivoting on toes of both feet, make a left about turn.

SIMULTANEOUSLY:
ii. Move arms up to split the hand-fist combination. Change right fist to hand and swing to the front, palm up.

iii. Swing left hand to the back, palm down. Eyes front.

b. From position (*a*):

i. Straighten right leg and kick to the front, keeping foot straight with leg.

SIMULTANEOUSLY:
ii. Change right hand to fist and return to ready position.

iii. Swing left hand up and to the front to clap right foot accurately, loud and clear. Eyes front.

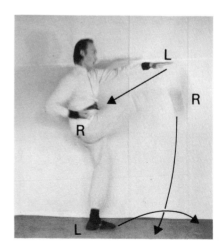

Finish

a. From previous position:

i. Land right foot in front of left foot.

ii. Pivoting on right foot, turn right and bring left foot up next to right foot.

SIMULTANEOUSLY:
iii. Change left hand to fist and return to ready position.

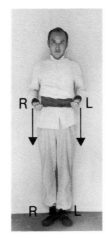

b. From position (*a*):

i. Change fists to hands and lower hands to stand at attention.

Power

The iron hand

This is a serious chapter. Serious because it deals with a problem that inevitably confronts the student at the very beginning of his studies; a problem that he knows so little about and is not capable of solving for himself. A wrong solution to this problem will lead to disaster. Therefore I demand care and attention when reading this chapter.

The World around us

It cannot be denied that everyone is impressed by the POWER that the *iron hand* possesses; the spectacular breaking and shattering of objects with unimaginable strength, its supremacy in combat. This *power* is frequently demonstrated clearly and attractively in films, television shows, magazines and story books. This magnificence of the iron hand is further confirmed in live demonstrations by masters and students of kung fu. The response to watching such performance usually ranges between excitement, pleasure, admiration, envy, jealousy and disbelief. Nevertheless, one thing is certain: everyone is impressed by it. The influence of What we see, hear and read of the iron hand can lead to a concept which is not complete and quite misleading. I refer this particularly to children and teenagers and those who know little of kung fu. The conception that often developes is that kung fu means breaking things and therefore if one can break things, one knows kung fu. The

truth is that kung fu does *not* only mean breaking things and that even if one can break things, that is not necessarily good kung fu. I have worked among thousands of children and teenagers and appreciate exactly how they feel. Most of us are not brought up under the influence of martial arts and have not received good training. It is natural, therefore, to behave instinctively until such time as the kung fu teacher has brought our minds to maturity.

There is one question that the student will inevitably have to face and will feel uncomfortable in answering. Soon enough, someone somewhere will ask, 'Can you break a brick?', 'Can you break a block of wood?', 'Can you break this?', 'Can you break that?'. The question often puts you on a spot because instinct tells you that if you say 'no' your influence may consequently suffer.

Among experts, there are differing opinions about the *iron hand*. The student should study them carefully and then decide just how far he will go.

Reasons for hand training

Apart from winning friends and influencing people, there are strong reasons why the hand should be trained:

(1) Without power, kung fu is useless. It can be compared to a blunt knife or a garden without flowers.

(2) It is a measure of one's progress in training. The degree of success in breaking objects shows the degree of

attainment in both speed and strength in relation to concentration and body control.

(3) Breaking practice is part of the course of training without which the training is not complete.

(4) A powerful hand reassures and gives confidence and satisfaction. Here is a true story. Once a girl got mad with her boy friend. She got so angry that she slapped him across the face. One hour later, she was still in the infirmary receiving treatment for her broken fingers.

Reasons against hand training

(1) For personal development: the learning of movements, keep you fit and provide recreation which does not require the hand being trained.

(2) For sport: contest rules do not allow contact blows so the hand *cannot* be used.

Reasons against heavy conditioning of hands

By heavy conditioning, we mean that the hand has reached an advanced stage of hardening. It can perform tasks as if it is made of iron.

(1) The heavily conditioned hand is calloused and not nice to look at. This process is irreversible.

(2) The hand cannot do delicate work.

(3) One tends to use more force than is necessary in the case of self-defence.

These three reasons are based on the difference between the social outlooks of our modern society and that of ancient China.

Weighing the importance of the iron hand in relation to one's way of life: at work, at home, with the family, with friends, and considering both the present and the future, the student must decide how far he will go in the training of his hands. It seems that *moderate conditioning* fits well into the jigsaw of modern living. By moderate conditioning we mean that the hand is trained for as long as it appears *natural*. By redesigning the training method, it is possible to acquire considerable power without the loss of dexterity of the hand. That is what the rest of this chapter is about. One may train both hands or just one hand alone.

The Tang method

The scene of iron hand training will not be unfamiliar to most of you. Over and over again, in clear, realistic and breath-taking ways it is shown on the screen. A giant bowl of sand is heated over fire. The hand is plunged into the scorching sand over and over again. As training progresses, more and more coarse sand is used until at the advanced stage the bowl contains gravel and stones. A scene like this, though impressive, sometimes gives the student a feeling of anxiety for where can he get such equipment? It is not convenient, even impossible, to have it at home. In kung fu classes, such equipment is not usually supplied. Where shall he go?

Certainly the method just described is a true method. It is a method the Shaolin monks used. It comes under the hard school. But it is not the only method. The *Tang method* is based on

	MODERN SOCIETY	ANCIENT CHINA
1	a calloused hand may not be socially attractive	a calloused hand was accepted
2	we may need our hands to do a great variety of work	martial artists could continue to specialise as a profession
3	the law and moral code do not allow the use of excess force in defense	the law was often the law of the strong and justice was brought about by revenge

principles of the soft school. It aims to strengthen and toughen the ligaments and tissues of the hand without affecting the appearance of the skin. The skin may possibly become slightly affected but the difference cannot be detected unless under close scrutiny. The method is specially tailored to suit modern living taking into account all aspects of life.

Let us take a good look at the hand. There are 5 striking areas.

1	palm heel	most powerful	takes least time to train
2	edge of hand	very powerful	takes a short time to train
3	the palm	quite powerful	takes longer time to train
4	back of hand	rather powerful	takes a long time to train
5	finger tips	least powerful	takes longest time to train

The palm heel and the edge of hand are the two most effective areas. Their power is way above that of the other three areas. So your first aim is to perfect the training of these two areas so that they can be put into use within a short period of time. The other three areas should also be trained simultaneously to strengthen the entire hand. But for breaking objects, the palm the back of the hand and the finger-tips cannot be ready until after a long period of training.

Bony Edge

Time—It is not possible to prescribe a fixed time for the completion of a certain stage of conditioning. Progress depends on (1) the initial physical state of the hand, ie. how soft or how hard the hand already is; (2) the time spent on its training; (3) the regularity of training; (4) determination; plus other psychological factors such as encouragement, pleasure and satisfaction.

Equipment—A bag about $1\frac{1}{2}$ feet long (45 cm), 1 foot wide (30 cm) and 2 to 3 inches thick (5 to 8 cm) is required. In deciding what material to use, we have to take into account our living environment. The most likely places for practice are those inside the house: the dining room, the kitchen, the bed-room, the hall, the landing and the living room (listed in descending order of frequency of use). Outdoor places like the garden are in fact rarely used due to (1) darkness at night; (2) cold and wind in winter; (3) rain. Therefore there is one thing which sooner or later will not be tolerated and that is the *spreading of dust*. Even if you can put up with it, someone else in the house will soon object and stop you. Anyway a dusty atmosphere is not desirable for exercise.

These days it is possible to find material which is dustproof such as leather, rubber, polythene and other man-made and synthetic materials. To cut costs and the trouble of making the bag, why not make use of an old brief-case or look around for a strong dust-proof bag that may have been thrown away as rubbish.

The *filling* is of three kinds according to the stage of training.

Stage i—This is the first stage when the hand is very soft and tender and liable to bruising and injury. The bag should be filled with a spongy or springy material of which *foam rubber* is ideal. The idea is to train the sensory nerve fibres of the hand to get used to the feeling of impact and to the increase in hand temperature and the increase of blood in the capillaries. Regular training once a day can complete this stage in one month.

Stage ii—Now the hand can withstand moderate bombardment and is not liable to bruising or injury. The filling of the bag is now a *semi-solid* material. Many things can be used, eg. pieces of carpet, carpet underlay, rubber sheets, door-mat, straw-mat, old blanket, newspapers. Give another month for a once-a-day regular training.

Stage iii—This is the final stage and there is no time limit. Students train for as long as they feel able. Now the filling is of solid hard material like wood boards, wood block, bricks and concrete block. The student may not need to use the bag. Instead, he can fix the hitting surface onto a solid wooden block. In this case the hitting surface will be a layer of one of the

semi-solid materials mentioned in stage ii.

Training Procedure

Warning—Only moderate force is required. There is no point in giving your hand bruises, lasting pain, swelling or even broken bones. This is contradictory to the objectives in training and hinders progress. It is inevitable that some minor bruising does occur, particularly during the early stages. When this happens, that part of the hand or the hand as a whole should rest from conditioning until it is well again.

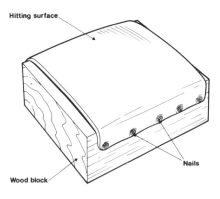

Duration—Because of the soft nature of the method, the hand is capable to withstand training for up to half an hour or more. And because of the flexible nature of the method, it is not necessary to work to a rigid time table. The student must decide on the duration of each session according to (1) how long his hand can withstand the beating; (2) how much time is available. Normally, however a session should not be less than 10 minutes.

Put the hitting bag on a strong table, stool, chair or other suitable place and stand in front of the bag.

Step 1—the palm
Raise hand to head height. Relax your shoulder and arm. Slap flat onto the bag to strike with the palm and fingers. In this case, the thumb must not bend into the palm.

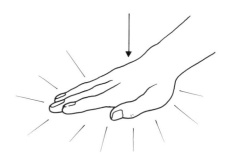

Step 2—the palm heel
Raise hand to head height. Arch the hand backwards and strike down to hit the bag with the palm heel. You may have the fingers straight if you prefer.

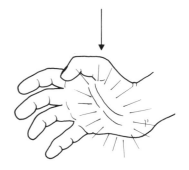

Step 3—edge of hand
Raise hand to head height. Form the hand properly with thumb bent. Concentrate on the striking point of the bag. Chop downwards with the edge of your hand. There should be no pain if your position is correct. If you feel pain, correct your striking position. You are either too high or too low; your hand is not vertical, or you strike with fingers or wrist bone. Use only the fleshy part of the edge.

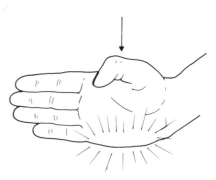

Step 4—back of hand
Raise hand to head height. Turn the palm up. Drop your hand to strike the bag with the back of the hand including the fingers.

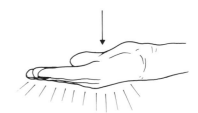

Step 5—finger-tips
Raise hand to head height. Form the hook in which fingers and thumb are pressed together to form a point. Keep your arm and shoulders relaxed. Turn the hook down and peck at the bag.

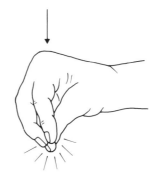

Step 6—the fist edge
Raise hand to head height. Clench the fist. Concentrate on the striking point of the bag. Hammer down and strike with the muscle edge of the fist.

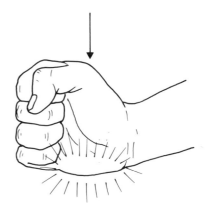

Step 7—the fist back

This is to train the large knuckle using the action of the backfist blow.

Raise fist to head height. Turn fist heart up. Strike down to deliver a backfist blow hitting the bag with the large knuckle of your fist.

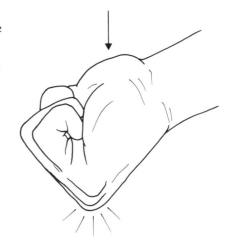

Step 8—the fist front

This is to train the two large knuckles using the action of the fist-front blow.

Raise fist to head height. Lift elbow. Turn fist heart towards you so that fist front is down. Plunge straight down to deliver a fist-front blow. Press shoulder down and add body weight to the blow with arm extended (not too hard at first). In the main use the two large knuckles as your striking area.

Repeat step 1 and continue until end of session.

The last 3 steps concern the fist. The fist edge is equivalent to the edge of hand in its power and strength in self-defence and in its effectiveness to break objects. The fist knuckles are the most powerful weapon of the fist. Try them and see. Hit your thigh using step 7 (the large knuckle) or step 8 (the two large knuckles). The power will penetrate deep into the flesh and you will appreciate the knuckles' great potential. (warning—to save you unnecessary pain and possible injury, hit yourself only lightly first, then gradually increase the force) Now use the same step 7 or 8 and hit a hard object such as a brick, table top or wooden chair. You will be amazed to find how lightly you have to strike if the pain is not to become unbearable. You will realize how useless the knuckles are (at this stage) in breaking things and you will not hesitate to use the edge of hand instead. And yet it is generally acknowledged that the

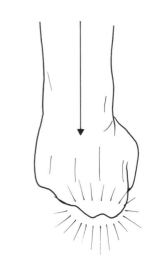

knuckles are extremely powerful even in breaking practice. How is that? Try to answer this question without reading the answer in the next paragraph.

The human body is covered with a layer of skin under which lie the muscles. These have the property of absorbing impact (but do not transmit impact). The thigh has a great volume of muscle. Therefore the fist can safely deliver a hard blow without receiving much reactive force. A hard object has no skin, no muscle. The *Law of Interaction* states that for every action there is an equal and opposite reaction. When striking the hard object, the knuckles receive considerable reactive force. What's more, the force is concentrated at the points of contact—the knuckles. The knuckles themselves are hard and not fleshy. Hence, unbearable pain and possible injury. What conclusion can we draw from this? The knuckles are powerful enough for defence. But for breaking practice, they need considerable conditioning. Once adequately trained, they can be extremely powerful indeed.

Medication?

It is possible to speed up progress with the use of a medication applied externally to the hands during training. Medication may come in many forms with either a cream base or alcohol base. There are problems with medication however. (1) such medication is not readily available everywhere; (2) even if one manages to get a supply of a medication, one cannot be sure of its reliability; (3) it costs money. (4) the recipe of such medication is handed down through many generations and is usually kept secret within a family or school. So the student will have no way of knowing what he is buying. Nevertheless, the functions of medication are:

(1) to help circulation of the blood so that swelling and bruising are reduced;

(2) to reduce pain;

(3) to increase the endurance of the hand against heavier beating;

(4) to speed up recovery from minor injuries.

A student wanting to use medication is advised to seek recommendation and guidance from a teacher as to (1) what to buy and (2) how to use. *Never experiment with chemicals*. To do so is childish, ignorant and dangerous. Always seek the experienced advice of a teacher.

The time machine (or how to live a 25-hour day)

Modern civilization gives us many things. It gives us electric power and electric light. The night is bright and we stay up late. Our waking life is lengthened. And yet we all face one problem: we just haven't got the time! The old masters practised 3 or 4 times a day. That certainly is out of the question now. We compromise by modifying our practice to once a day. 80% of students still find this too demanding. A two hour practice session is gradually cut down to 1 hour; 30 minutes; then to 15 minutes. Students attending classes once a week drop out simply because they can't manage the time! Often, we read in newspapers and magazines of firms offering '5 minutes a day' courses of physical exercise—another proof of time starvation in modern living.

The fact remains that we do not get something for nothing. What we get is what we put in. If it took an old master 3 times a day for 3 years to achieve a certain skill, is it not silly or unreasonable to expect the same achievement by working 1 hour, once a week, for 6 months? Is it not natural that progress would be slow? The result is that the student gradually (1) loses faith in himself; (2) loses faith in the method; (3) loses interest and (4) gives up. This is sad when one considers the enthusiasm with which he started.

There is no short cut to learning, just as there is no short cut to growing up. A person must go through so much physically and mentally before he is grown up (and some people never do grow up, mentally at least). So the hand must receive a lot of attention before it is matured and ready. If there is a so called short cut then it should be more properly defined as 'a more effective method' or 'a better organised method' or 'a time saving method'.

The spirit of a kung fu student must be positive and constructive. There must be a way. We now know that the more we put in the more we get out. The greatest challenge is PERSEVERANCE. Can we see ourselves through and win?

That is why I have devised and now offer to you this *Time Machine Approach* tailored to suit contemporary living. The *machine* is yourself. The *time* is time saved during the day and evening, which normally would have been wasted. No equipment is required and the Approach can be practised anytime, anywhere and for any duration.

The hour is made up of 60 minutes and the minute of 60 seconds. A few seconds here and a few minutes there soon add up to the hour. During each day of your life, there are 101 instances when time can be saved and made use of. Waiting for a friend, waiting for the bus, waiting for the kettle to boil, waiting for the bathroom, during the bus or train journey, going up and down stairs, watching an uninteresting television programme or a programme which does not need much concentration, or that you have been sitting and watching for so long that you need a stretch are some typical examples. If a student finds it hard to put aside half an hour or 15 minutes for a training session, he will now be amazed to find that he can have up to 1 hour's extra training during his working day by using the Time Machine Approach.

Approach 1—edge of hand against palm heel

(The photographs show the edge of the right hand against the left palm heel.) Stand your right hand up with thumb bent and edge down, (vertical chopping position). Stretch your left hand out with thumb straight and palm heel up facing edge of right hand, (fingers straight or slightly bent). Turn the edge of your hand in line with palm heel so that the hands are at right angle (90°), (Photo 1).

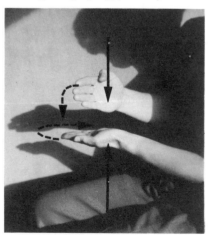

Chop the edge of your hand down and lift the palm heel up so that they both strike each other. Use moderate force and do not cause pain.

While hitting, gradually turn right hand clockwise (away from you) and left hand anti-clockwise (towards you) until the right hand is horizontal (palm up) delivering horizontal chops towards the left. The left hand is now vertical (standing up) delivering palm heel strikes towards the right. The two hands are again at right angle (Photo 2).

Continue the training, gradually turning the hands back again to the starting position of photo 1. The cycle is repeated and keeps repeating as long as time allows or until you have enough.

Thus you see, every strike trains both hands at once in two different places.

Approach 2—palm heel against palm heel

Stretch both hands in front of you vertically, thumbs up, edges down and

palm facing palm as if clapping hands (photo 3). Fingers straight.

Strike palm heel against palm heel.

While striking, gradually turn right hand up and left hand down until the fingers point towards opposite directions and in a straight line (photo 4). The

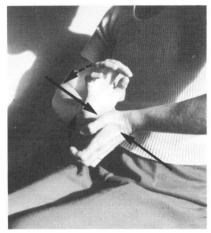

tension of the palm heel muscles can now be assisted by bending and tensing the fingers.

Now continue striking and gradually turn right hand down and left hand up, pass the starting position of photo 3, and continue turning until the right hand fingers are vertically down and the left hand fingers are vertically up (photo 5).

Do not forget to tense the fingers to help create tension in the palm heels.

To complete the cycle, gradually turn right hand up and left hand down to the starting position shown in photo 3. Fingers straight again. Repeat cycle.

Approach 3—knuckles against knuckles
Hit lightly first, then gradually increase strength. Clench fists. Put right fist over left fist knuckles facing knuckles. (photo 6).

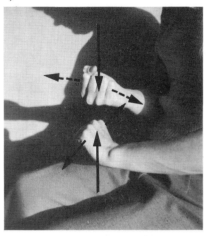

Close up fists to strike knuckles against knuckles. Shift fists in and out in opposite directions (right fist in and left fist out; right fist out and left fist in) so that each knuckle in turn hits all the knuckles of the other hand. Train also the surrounding area, the fist at the front and the fist at the back of the knuckles.

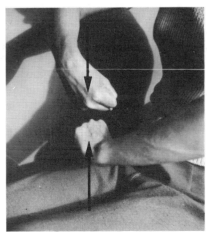

Change positions and put left fist over right fist and repeat above.

Now with the right fist on top again, fist heart towards you, the knuckle lines are crossed at right angle (photo 7). Strike with the fist front of right knuckles against all areas of the left fist knuckles.

Change positions with left fist on top and repeat. The cycle is completed.

Approach 4—fist edge against fist front

Clench fists, right fist heart up with fist edge facing left fist front. Left fist heart is down (photo 8).

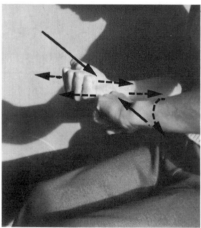

Hammer fist edge against fist front. Shift fists in and out in opposite directions to make sure that all areas are struck.

Turn left fist heart up and continue hammering left fist front with right fist edge.

Change positions to hammer right fist front with left fist edge.

Approach 5—fingertips

Do not expect the fingertips to be able to break anything, not for a long time yet. The idea of this exercise is to strengthen the fingers and their tips which are useful in defence and also to give the other hand the experience of sharp shocks caused by the pecking of the fingertips.

Photo 9 shows the right hook pecking at the left palm. I suggest the hook should peck the left hand all over, palm and back including fingers. Repeat the same with left hook against right hand.

One variation of this approach is to use the spear hand instead of the hook. A further variation is to use the fingers individually and the index finger and middle finger in pair spread out to a V-shape.

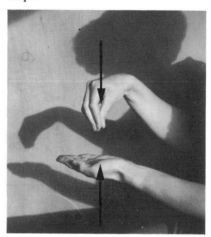

Approach 6—hand exercise

The idea of this exercise is to keep the hand particularly fingers in a healthy, fit and flexible condition. And to ensure that its dexterity is not impaired through over conditioning.

The method is to bend the fingers and hand inwards as well as backwards to the extreme with the help of the other hand.

a. Photo 10 shows the right thumb

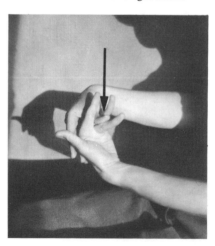

helping the left middle finger to bend fully inwards at the base knuckle joint. With a little pressure from the thumb, a cracking sound is made by the joint. (This is usually the case though it is not necessary to have the sound.) There are 14 finger joints in each hand. Do the same to all 14 joints.

b. Photo 11 shows the right thumb and index finger helping to press back the left

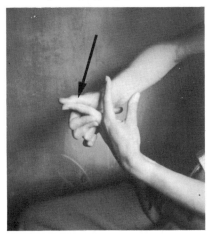

middle finger as far as possible at the base knuckle joint. Do the same to all 14 joints.

c. Photo 12 shows the right fist wheel securing the tip of the left middle finger.

By turning the fist and left hand in opposite directions back and forth, the finger is twisted in alternating directions. Do the same to all five fingers.

d. With right hand, grip hold of left hand by the back, squeeze left hand in as much as possible bending at the wrist.

e. With right hand, grip hold of left hand by the palm, push and squeeze the left hand backwards as much as possible bending at the wrist.

f. Repeat the above to the right hand helping with the left hand.

The hard school

For the sake of completeness, I have included here a method from the hard school, which is practicable at home. Because it is a hard school method, its aim is to toughen and roughen the hand from the outside. I must warn that any student wanting to experiment with this method must watch his skin closely and stop when the desired thickening of the skin has been achieved. This method, though simple, can condition the hand to the extreme and is quick to do so. Again, a student must consider the pros and cons before he goes beyond moderate conditioning.

The method is similar to that described at the beginning of this chapter except that heat is not used. It is particularly useful for fingertips.

Equipment—a container large enough to accommodate the entire hand (not less than 1 foot or 30 cm deep) eg. a bin, a bucket, a big tin or a large plant pot (seal the hole at the bottom). Fill the container with material according to the following stages:

moderate 1: rice or similar grain
moderate 2: dry beans or peas (traditionally, Chinese green and black beans are used. These may not be obtainable. Substitute with readily available beans or peas.)
moderate 3: fine sand
extreme 1: coarse sand
extreme 2: gravel
extreme 3: small stones

Action—Form the hand (in this case, do not bend thumb). Lift hand to chest height, fingertips pointing at container. Aim at the centre of container. Plunge and dive the hand right into the material until wrist deep. Pull hand out and repeat. Train the other hand if required.

That's that. Very simple. Yet, very effective.

Break testing

Break testing is necessary because:
1. It checks and measures our progress in training;
2. It is part of the training itself. This is because:

(*a*) the hand needs the experience of actually hitting and breaking hard objects. As mentioned earlier, there is a difference between hitting a human body and hitting a hard object because the latter has no muscle or skin. The hand needs to get used to the feeling of the sharp shock of impact before the object is broken. And, above all, if the object is not broken;

(*b*) breaking technique is an art in itself which can best be developed through actual practice.

Warning—It is here that most accidents occur—bruises, swellings, pain, broken bones, disheartening loss of confidence. These are caused by over-ambition and an impatience to progress quickly, backed by courage and a daring spirit of adventure. (Courage and spirit of adventure are good things but are badly used without the guidance of reason.) Also, a student will often come across objects the strength of which he under-estimates, eg. he takes a walk over the hill and finds a broken branch of a tree. He has a go at it and, bang—injury!

So, aim at gradual progress and persevere—keep on. Be careful. There is no need to hurt yourself (though minor bruises are inevitable and therefore expected.)

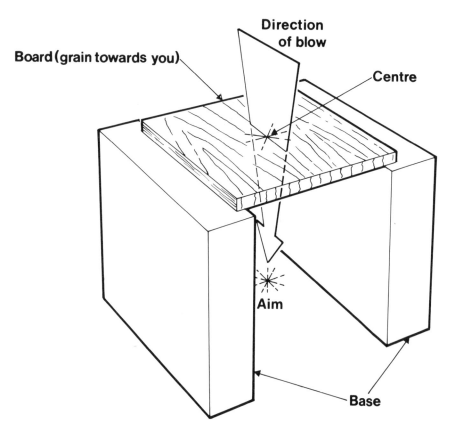

Material—The best material for break testing is wooden boards. Start with thin boards ($\frac{3}{4}$ or $\frac{1}{2}$ inch boards). You can start testing right from the beginning of hand training. As you progress, you either (1) increase the thickness of the board or (2) put 2 or 3 etc. boards together. The time will come when you can break a 2 or 3 inch board. Then you can try a brick. If you can find other material which can give you progressive testing like boards, you can use it also.

A matter of economy—In the course of your training, you will have broken hundreds of boards, probably a thousand. If you have to buy them, it will cost you a small fortune. That's why I have not standardised the size of the board although usually 12 inch square boards are used.

Here is one way that will save you money. Start with a board of suitable size (about 12 inch square or rectangle). Place it on a base (this can be 2 chairs, 2 stools, 2 tables, 2 piles of bricks, etc.) The grain of the board should run towards you.

Action

  i. Locate the centre of the board.

  ii. Practise the hitting movement 2 or 3 times, striking only to touch the centre (—a warming-up exercise to put you in the right state of mind and also to make sure your entire body position is *absolutely accurate*—a vital factor).

  iii. Aim 4 inches below the centre of the board and concentrate on this point.

  iv. Raise hand with a deep breath.

  v. Strike downwards vertically and release your breath with a shout (any sound will do).

The first hand positions to be used are (1) palm heel, (2) edge of hand, (3) fist edge.

The next position to be ready for use is (4) the fist front (two large knuckles).

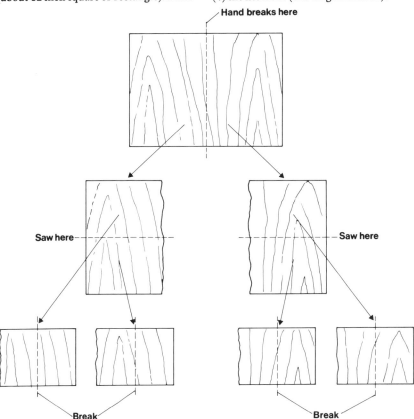

Hand breaks here

Saw here

Saw here

Break

Break

This is followed by (5) the fist back (large knuckle).

The other three positions: (6) the palm (7) the back of hand and (8) the fingertips. These will not be ready for a long time. When they are ready, you will be in the advanced stage of your training.

Now back to the matter of economy. So you have broken a board. What to do with it now? Throw it away?

You can do one of two things or both:

1. Try to break each half again. If you succeed, break each quarter again and so on. *But* as the half, the quarter, the eighth, etc. become narrower and narrower, they also become harder and harder to break and the time will come when you cannot break them anymore.

2. Saw the half, quarter, eighth, etc. across the grain to make them smaller. You will find they still give you good practice. A board reduced to the size of 3 or 4 inch square or rectangle is still usable. After that, you can throw it away, or still keep it for practising with the knuckles. In this way, you get maximum value of the board.

Obviously, it is hard to check and measure progress if the board size changes all the time. For this purpose, periodically, you need to set yourself a standard size and, even better, using the same kind of wood. In this way, accurate measurement can be made by the increase in thickness of the board or the increase in number of the same boards broken with the same strike. If your aim is to break bricks at a later stage, one idea is to saw your board to the size of a brick (but much thinner of course). Then gradually increase thickness until it is comparable to that of the brick. Then you can try the brick.

Note: When you use the palm heel and particularly when the board has become very small, it is better if you move to the front of a base so that the board grain now runs across you. This is because the striking area of the palm heel runs across the base of the palm. In this position, the striking area will be in line with the grain and the effect of the strike is much greater.

In terms of economy, it is best if you do not need to pay for the material at all. That is why, again, I have not standardised the kind of wood to be used.

BASE

You are here

There are pieces of wood, planks, boards, blocks, broken doors, old furniture etc. lying about everywhere. If you look around, you will find them. Saw them up to a good size for practice. And do not be put off by the thought of sawing. Sawing is very good training for your arm, shoulder and abdominal muscles. Spare the trouble, spoil the chance! A good old saw can do you as much good as a body-building exerciser.

Bricks—These days bricks are made with a great variety of substances. They come in different colours, sizes and designs. All I am concerned with is for you to realize that some bricks are easier to break than others. Also that a brick which has been left outside to weather, particularly in a wet condition, will weaken and hence be easier to break. Choose the kinds of bricks which have simple flat surfaces for striking (not all kinds of bricks are simple and flat surfaced).

There are 2 ways of breaking a brick. The first way is identical to that I described in breaking boards.

The second way is more difficult and you should not try it until you have been successful with the first.

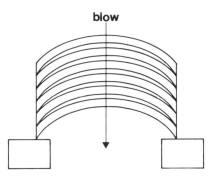

blow

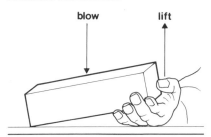

blow   **lift**

i. Support one end of the brick with one hand.

ii. Locate centre of brick.

iii. Practise hitting movement 2 or 3 times.

iv. Aim below the centre and concentrate on that point.

v. Raise the other hand with a deep breath inwards.

vi. Strike down vertically and release breath with a shout.

vii. Simultaneously, lift the supporting hand upwards.

(In terms of economy one has got to be resourceful. Anything which is readily available and free for the taking should be made use of. Apart from saving money, you will find it more interesting to be breaking different things and gaining wider experience.)

Stack pile—This is an impressive display of skill. Curved materials, eg. tiles, are ideal. When such materials are not available, flat materials can also be used if they are separated as shown. You must be able to sustain power right through to the end. Each layer is broken separately but in quick succession (that is the idea of the gaps). With practice, you will find you can break quite a few layers

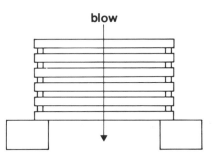

blow

this way. The sustainment (or continued flow) of power can best be achieved with the help of the body. While keeping the arm rigid, press down continuously with the body.

Pattern of development—What will be happening to you is this. At first, your hand will be tender and soft. It will not be able to stand the impact against a hard object. It hurts. Therefore you cannot strike very hard and you will break only thin boards or weak objects. This means that your arm, shoulder and body use only part of their strength. At this stage, *technique* will not seem to mean very much to you because if you hit harder things, your hand hurts.

Gradually, as you make progress, the hand will begin to catch up with your strength. Now you can strike as hard as you want because the hand can take it. Then something strange happens. One day you can break two boards. Another day you cannot. You will begin to think that you will never break three boards. Somehow, one day, you will do it. Yet you cannot do it again. You are puzzled? That is what happens when the operation demands maximum power and you lack skill (or breaking technique). That is the time when strength has to be used to its *maximum* advantage. No bit of power cannot be wasted. Now is the time that all the principles discussed in the last chapter (Force and Motion) come into play. All these questions have to be answered:

Why is that the blow has to be perpendicular to the surface of the target? (resolution of forces)
How can the body help? (forces acting in a straight line)
How important is speed? (law of acceleration. This is extremely important. Maximum speed gives maximum force.)

Read the last chapter again and see if you can give yourself satisfactory answers.

Even more surprising things are yet to come. As the hand matures, you will feel able to hit anything. It does not hurt any more. You decide to break something (say a brick). You strike. Your hand is fine. But the brick does not move. How is that? You lack strength. This will come if you keep practising, trying and doing the Sequences.

The modern approach
The one reason why modern civilization can progress at such a rapid pace is that we approach education and learning in a more effective manner than our predecessors and our attitude towards knowledge is more broad-minded. We have come to understand that among the various disciplines of learning, there is common ground, and that one discipline can no longer be isolated from the others. We make use of this understanding to devise systems that allow one discipline to help another. That is how we can learn so much in so short a time. A baby is born new and fresh. Yet within a few decades he may be able to invent spacecrafts that probe outer space.

In ancient times, a student who attended a martial arts school or followed a master, came straight from his home with little training or education of any kind. Communication (particularly the printing of books) and transport were

very poor. This meant that the flow of knowledge was near to standing-still. So the school and masters had to provide their own system. And the system had to be complete and self-contained so that the new student could be built up from nothing to perfection. Because such a system was a full course of education, it demanded time. But then time was no problem.

Now we have compulsary and free education up to the teenage years. Communications and transport are efficient. The flow of knowledge is continuous and accelerating (the fact that you are reading this book is one example). The school provides a complete course of education to bring a child up to be widely accomplished (physically, mentally and spiritually). Without you knowing, you have already received a great part of the teaching you could have expected from the old master.

Let us first look into our school. A kung fu student needs to be accomplished spiritually too, for the mind is the master of the body. Compare the body to a knife and the mind to the hand that uses the knife. If the hand does not use the knife properly, it will damage the knife or use it to commit an offence. This part of our training is provided in the Religious Education provided in school. Many children do not take it seriously. A young kung fu student, I hope, from now on, will develop a better attitude.

Mental health and soundness are also important. This training is being looked after by the various departments in school, which offer many different subjects of study and employing modern teaching methods to exercise the mind.

Obviously, a kung fu student demands a great deal physically. Long ago, he used to spend hours every day, training his body, doing the recommended exercises and completing tasks assigned by his master. (This practice, as mentioned earlier, is regarded as impossible by many students today *simply because they have not got the TIME!*) Little does a student know that such training is already provided for in school! We have physical education classes. We play games. We use athletics and gymnastics. There is a lot of ground in common between our physical education and kung fu. High jump and long jump prepare you for the flying kick. Football, basketball, tennis, etc. all give overall training to body and limbs. Some schools teach judo, boxing and fencing which brings you a bit nearer to kung fu. In short, if you work at being good at physical education in school, you have done the basic training and you are already half way to being a success at kung fu. So take another look at physical education.

Now let us look outside school. Again, there are many activities through which you can benefit, eg. swimming, cycling, walking. For those who are too young to be admitted to a kung fu club (also for grown-ups), there is one class (or club) I can recommend which has direct relationship to kung fu and which has no minimum age requirement. That is practical YOGA. And you don't have to aim to specialize in it. Essential basic training will be good enough. Alternatively, fencing gives good training. Dancing gives very good exercise. Ballroom dancing, Latin-American dancing which is very demanding and above all, the ballet. Ballet training can be very successfully employed to develop kung fu techniques.

It is impossible to list and discuss all related activities. A few examples have been given here. With understanding and common sense you can go from here. Modern civilization has given us rich living with plenty to do. While enjoying this great variety of opportunities, it is possible to enrich life even further by letting one opportunity help another. In this way, there is no need to give up something for the sake of another. This great variety can link together to form a network, based on common ground, which may even prove to be very desirable and well worth having. This works on the principle of 'killing two birds with one stone'. Not only the *time* problem is solved but also our progress can advance by leaps and bounds. Such is the modern approach to kung fu.

Force and motion

Force and Motion

IT IS NEVER too early to start thinking 'Why?' and 'How?'. In fact, it is imperative that every student should do so because understanding is the life of learning. Without understanding, learning is dead. With it, learning is alive but also grows bigger and stronger. That is what we call creativity. The student is able to create something of his own out of what is given to him so that he ends up having more than he has received. This is how we learn:

1. The decline of ability with age depends upon the subject to be learned. This means that one should not say, 'I'm too old. I've had it. I've passed learning.' It depends upon the subject. Given a suitable subject, one can learn just as well no matter how old. On the other hand, if the subject is unsuitable, one cannot learn no matter how young.

2. A motivated learner acquires knowledge more readily. A learner in possession of this book has shown enough motivation to satisfy this condition.

3. Learning under the control of reward is usually preferable. Reward includes self-satisfaction, the awareness of success, ability to appreciate, having a good time, influencing friends, making friends, approval by others, ability to create and encouragement.

4. Tolerance of failure is best taught through providing a backlog of success that compensates for the failures. 'Failure is the mother of success.' To make sure that one does not fail again, he must find out WHY he failed.

5. Meaningful material and meaningful tasks are learned more readily than nonsense material and tasks. Therefore the learner must UNDERSTAND what he is doing.

6. There is no substitute for repetitive practice in the learning of skills. One must practise regularly.

7. Information about a good performance, knowledge of mistakes and knowledge of success, aid learning.

8. Transfer of learning, i.e., to apply the knowledge gained from one area to another area, will be better if the learner can discover relationships for himself.

9. Spaced recalls, i.e., periodic revision, are advantageous for retaining learning for a long time.

10. Learning is the establishing of new associations with past experience. Past experience together with new learning, produce knowledge that can be retained.

UNITS: For our purposes, quantitative units such as the kilogram for mass and the newton for force will not be quoted in our discussions so as not to confuse.

Forces acting in a straight line

One good example of this is the contest 'tug-of-war'. The team with a greater force will pull the other team over. Let us

suppose that team A has a force of 10 and
team B 9. Then team A will win by a force
of 10–9=1.

One interesting thing to note is that the
same effect could be produced by
replacing the teams with one boy pulling
the rope in the winning direction with a
force of 1. This shows that forces can be
subtracted from one another. The net
force is called the resultant force.

Forces can be added together as well. If
a car breaks down and one man tries to
push it with a force of 5. Man B comes to
help and also pushes with a force of 5.
Now the combined force, i.e., resultant
force, moves the car along. 5 + 5 = 10.
Man C comes and offer to tow with his
car. Naturally, the same effect can be
produced and A and B do not need to push
anymore.

In Kung Fu, the same principle applies.
We can add and subtract forces. In
making an attack, we often say, 'Back it
up with the body weight.' Very often, an
attack occurs when the attacker is
advancing in the same direction. Now we
know that this is because the
weight of the body and the forward
motive force of the body can be added to
the force of a punch, chop or kick, making
the attack much more powerful.

'How to put this principle to practice' is
a technical question. Consider movement
6 of sequence 2 'κ HAND STRIKE'. (Look it
up now!) You are to strike with the edge
of your left hand straight forward to, e.g.,
opponent's collarbone. How can you add
forces to your forward striking hand?

i. Why do you simultaneously return right fist to ready position? Is it that you only want the right fist to be ready for the next action? No, not only that. The returning of right fist and out going of left hand should rotate your body in the direction of attack, i.e., clockwise, so that AT THE MOMENT OF IMPACT, the right shoulder is backward and the left shoulder is forward. From the left shoulder, the weight of the body (or the power of the twisting of the body) is transmitted through the arm to the hand. Now:

Resultant Force = Force of hand + Force of body

ii. You are also asked to turn right, advance left foot one step and form the left bow stance. Why? Is it that you want to gain distance? Yes, but there is more. The advancing left foot causes the body to move and movement means force. This force is in the same direction as the attack and therefore can be added. So this body motive force is transmitted through the left shoulder and the arm to the hand. Then:

Resultant Force = Force of hand + Force of body + Motive force

Remember we are dealing with forces acting in a straight line. Any force perpendicular to this straight line has no contribution.

3 steps in one go (e.g., opponent keeps a distance from you). Then you will be up and down like a yo-yo. To avoid this, you can practise pushing feet and body into the ground with every advance.

Which is a better hammer, an iron one or a rubber one? Without hesitation, you will answer, 'The iron one.' Why? 'Because force from the arm can be transmitted completely through the RIGID iron hammer to hit the target.' Similarly, for transmission, addition and delivery of forces, every part of the body should be rigid AT THE MOMENT OF IMPACT. To do this, you need to tense the muscles of hands or fists, arms, shoulders, body, hips, legs and foot.

Why emphasize THE MOMENT OF IMPACT? That is the most important moment of the whole operation. That is the moment which decides whether your operation has succeeded or failed and everything counts at that moment. If the moment shows success, all that you have done before has been worthwhile. If it shows failure, then, no matter how good a show you have put on before that moment, it has no value.

Consider the movement that follows, i.e., movement 7 of sequence 2. (Look it up!) This time you keep the same left bow stance, change left hand to fist and return to ready position and simultaneously change right fist to hand and strike forward. Notice anything? What is the

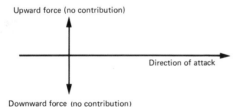

Upward force (no contribution)

Direction of attack

Downward force (no contribution)

So, when you advance your left foot, do not raise the body upwards to drop downwards again. If you do, you will (a) waste energy, (b) waste time, (c) disturb balance, (d) disturb the straight line and (e) have less striking power. This is particularly so in real combat when circumstances require you to advance 2 or

effect of the 'in' of left fist and 'out' of right hand? It helps the body to rotate anticlockwise IN THE DIRECTION OF THE STRIKE so that AT THE MOMENT OF IMPACT your right shoulder is forward. Then:

Resultant force = Force of hand + Force of body

The resultant force gives a very powerful strike.

Any other example? What about movements 1, 2, 3, 11, 20, 27 of sequence 1; movements 2, 5, 17, 19, 21, 23 of sequence 2 and more from sequence 3.

If you do everything in the opposite direction, you will, of course, have subtraction of forces. This, in the case of attack, is undesirable. If, for instance, in the K HAND STRIKE, you twist your body away from the direction of attack and also stepping backward, then:

Resultant force = Force of hand − Force of body − Motive force

Can subtraction of forces be advantageous? Yes.

i. When you are under attack and there is no way of blocking, then jump immediately out of the straight line of attack, i.e., jump to the side. If you succeed, you have reduced the attack to nothing. If, however, this is not possible, and the only way out is to jump backward, then do so with the greatest speed (i.e., force). Then:

Impact = Attacking force − Motive force

If motive force = attacking force; then impact = O, meaning you and opponent moving at the same speed in the direction of attack and you suffer no harm.

If motive force is greater than attacking force, then impact is negative, meaning you are moving faster away from opponent and suffer no harm.

This throws light on the danger of your opponent succeeding to deliver a blow when you are advancing. This is often the case when you advance to attack but stopped by the blow before your final stage of attack is reached. So

Impact = Attacking force + Motive force

and you suffer greatly. To prevent this happening, always get the hand, which is not used for attack, ready to block any blow that may come your way.

ii. The subtraction of forces helps to

withdraw your attacking hand or foot quickly by subtracting out all forward going forces. This is necessary AFTER your blow is completed. The reasons are (a) you can repeat the blow if necessary; (b) it brings you back to a well-balanced position quickly.

Resolution of forces

Imagine you punch straight at a wall, i.e., 90° to the wall. The wall will receive full force from your punch.

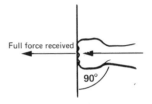

Full force received

90°

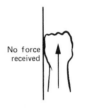

No force received

If you punch along the surface of the wall, i.e., at 0° to the wall, your punch will have no effect to the wall. These are two extreme cases. What if you punch at 45° to the wall? Say, you use a force of 10. This force can be resolved into two components, one parallel to the surface of the wall and one perpendicular to it. At 45°, the two components are equal. In this case, it works out to be approximately 7 each. The parallel component has no effect to the wall. So the wall is hit as if by a head-on force of 7 and, of course, receives the full force of 7.

The resolution of a force can easily be done graphically in the following way:

i. Draw the surface to be hit, (a straight line).

ii. Choose a convenient scale (e.g., 1 cm for 1 unit of force) and draw a line of force at the appropriate angle to the surface (the dotted line of 10 in the above diagram).

iii. From the end of the line of force, drop a line perpendicular to the surface and another line parallel to it, (the two dotted lines).

iv. From the other end of the line of force that touches the surface, drop the two components, one parallel to and one perpendicular to the surface, to meet the previous two lines (dotted lines). Now you have constructed a rectangle or a square (as in the case of 45° punch).

v. By measuring the length of the components and converting back to units of force according to scale, their magnitude can be found.

Let us see what happens if you punch 30° to the wall. The perpendicular component shows only a force of 5 and that is what the wall receives.

But at 60° the perpendicular component is increased to 8.7. So the angle of attack makes a great difference to the impact. The ideal angle is 90°. The smaller the angle, the weaker is the impact.

What enlightenment can this give to the practice of Kung Fu?

i. You should aim to strike target in a perpendicular direction.
ii. Avoid being hit in a perpendicular direction. Of course, you should avoid being hit at all. However, if you are unfortunate enough to let your defence be broken and to let in a blow, a last trick you can do is to turn that part of your body in a direction so as to make the skin parallel to the direction of attack. Given speed, it is possible to nullify the attack but it must be stressed that you need a great deal of experience to do this.

iii. Is it possible that when you have blocked an attack, you still suffer injury?

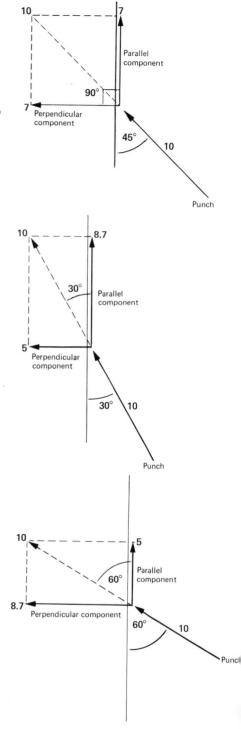

Sadly, yes. Why? Your blocking limb, usually the arm, has received a great proportion of the blow, e.g., elbow joint, fingers. This can only happen when the arm makes a big angle with the incoming force. This is particularly so when the attack comes in a circular or roundhouse fashion, e.g., level chop or edge of hand chop, the hammer blow or roundhouse kick. So the general rule of blocking is not to stop the incoming force head-on but to approach it from the side and deflect its direction.

Centre of gravity

THE CENTRE OF GRAVITY of any object, including the body, is that point at which all of its weight may be considered to be concentrated.

Let us find out. Take a piece of cardboard and draw the outline of a man. in standing position. Cut it out. Take a pin and pin the shape onto a vertical surface (say the side of a box) through any point (say a point in the head). Swing the shape freely and let it come to rest. Drop a plumb line from the pin. You can use a piece of thread and tie a small weight at one end of it. Then draw a line along the plumb line. (See diagram a.)

Next suspend the shape from another point (say the hip) and draw another line along the plumb line (diagram b). Now you will find that this line intersects the previous line. The point of intersection is the centre of gravity.

It is sufficient to use two lines to find the centre of gravity. In order to check the results and as a matter of interest, you may do it again from a third point (the shoulder). Again, the third line intersects at the same point (diagram c). You may continue this experiment for as many more times as you like and you will find that all lines intersect at the same point— the centre of gravity.

So for this standing model, the centre of gravity is in the abdomen. Put the point of a pencil directly beneath the centre of gravity—the shape is balanced.

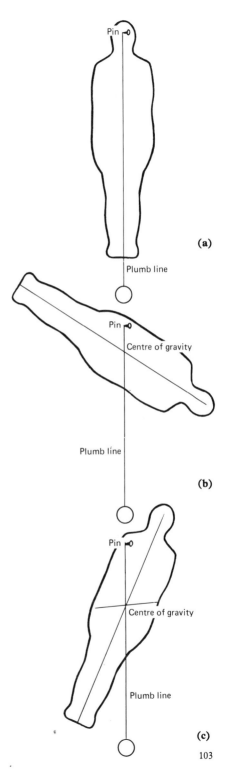

103

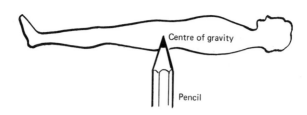

Centre of gravity

Pencil

Let us do the experiment on a model of the horse stance.

This time the centre of gravity is in the abdomen and just slightly higher up than that of the standing model. But the distance of it from the ground is SHORTER due to the bending of the knees and that is an important point to remember.

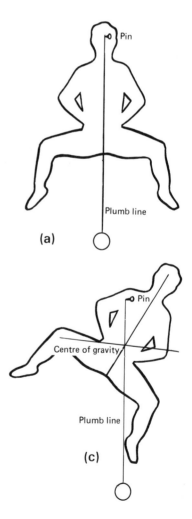

Pin

Plumb line

(a)

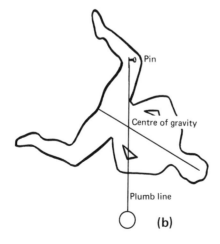

Pin

Centre of gravity

Plumb line

(b)

Pin

Centre of gravity

Plumb line

(c)

Let us try the bow and arrow stance.
Also try the L stance.

The centre of gravity has shifted to the
side of the stretched leg, more so in the L
stance. So any part of the body which
sticks out has the influence of pulling the
centre of gravity towards it. This happens
when we deliver a punch and particularly
so when we kick. The centre of gravity is
nearest to the ground in the L stance
simply because the body is at its lowest
position.

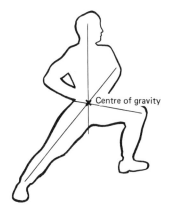

So, what have we learned? The body
weight may be considered to be
concentrated at the centre of gravity. This
centre is not a fixed point in the body but
moves according to the body posture. Any
part of the body which sticks out can pull
the centre towards it. The centre can be
lowered or raised along with the body. So
when we fight and when the body is
moving in many directions, we expect the
centre to be moving accordingly. These
are very important elements in the study
of balance and stability which we will see
in a moment.

The centre of gravity does not
necessarily lie within the body. It can be
outside the body. Consider the letters L,
Q, U, O, D, J, C and V. Cut out shapes of
them and find out for yourself. In the
course of movement, the body may at one
time fit into one of those shapes. Then the
centre will lie outside the body.

Stability and balance

Remember this most important rule: THE
LARGER THE BASE OF THE BODY AND THE
LOWER ITS CENTRE OF GRAVITY, THE MORE
STABLE IS THE BODY.

First, let us define stability. The body is
stable if the plumb line dropped from the
centre of gravity falls within the area of
the base.

Therefore, a man in standing position
is stable (diagram a overpage).

In stable equilibrium, the body has the
tendency to return itself to its original
position if a force is applied to alter that
position slightly (diagram b overpage).

If the force has altered the position to
such that the plumb line falls upon the
edge of the base, then the body becomes

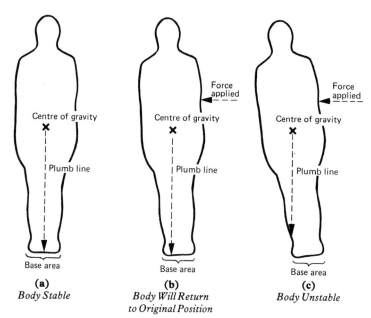

(a)
Body Stable

(b)
*Body Will Return
to Original Position*

(c)
Body Unstable

unstable. It will either return to its original position or fall over (diagram c).

If, however, the force is strong enough to make the plumb line fall outside the base area, the body will fall into a new position of stable equilibrium. It will not return to the original position (diagrams d & e).

On the one hand, it is unfortunate that you should choose to stand as in diagram (a). The lying position of diagram (e) is a much more stable one due to its large base area and low centre of gravity. On the other hand, it is a good thing that your opponent should also choose to stand. It is up to you to make the most of both situations.

To go a little further into the mechanics of overturning a body, we must understand that a body cannot be overturned unless its centre of gravity is first raised. This is because in any stable

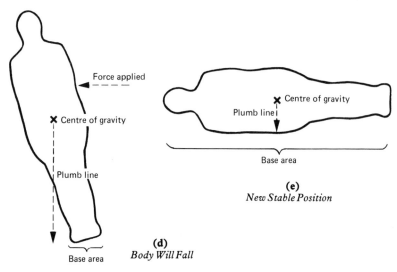

(e)
New Stable Position

(d)
Body Will Fall

position, the centre is at its lowest for that position. The body has to go through the stages of stable—unstable—fall. From the stable stage to the unstable stage, the centre of gravity has to be raised.

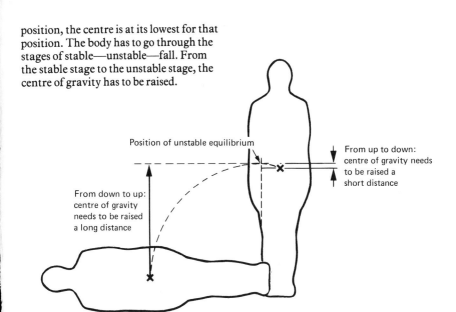

Position of unstable equilibrium

From up to down: centre of gravity needs to be raised a short distance

From down to up: centre of gravity needs to be raised a long distance

A study of the above diagram explains and leads us to the important understanding that although many positions are stable positions, their DEGREE OF STABILITY differs. The moving body tends to favour a more stable position though not always to our advantage. One good example is the kick. Once the kicking leg is sent forward, not only the base area is reduced to that of the standing foot, but also the kicking leg pulls the centre of gravity along with it. On top of these is the reactive force of the impact. So this position is the least stable position and it is nature's design that the body tends to favour a more stable one, e.g., to fall down (not to our advantage). Therefore, we must overcome this tendency by providing an alternative in the following way: i. kick with speed to reduce time; ii. snap kicking foot back

immediately after completion; iii. land kicking foot as soon as possible; iv. balance with arms and body.

The degree of stability can be judged by the rule mentioned at the beginning of this section:
THE LARGER THE BASE OF THE BODY AND THE LOWER ITS CENTRE OF GRAVITY, THE MORE STABLE IS THE BODY.

When the feet are apart as in the horse stance, the base area is the area described by the feet (the shaded area in the diagram).

Whenever the feet are apart, the base area always take up a long and narrow shape. It is easier for the centre of gravity to move sideways to the outside of the base area and to cause a fall. The distance is much shorter to travel. That is why in most cases, force is applied along the straight line of the feet.

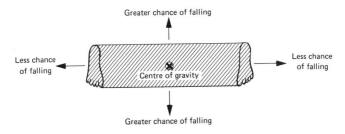

Greater chance of falling

Less chance of falling

Centre of gravity

Less chance of falling

Greater chance of falling

The law of inertia

It states that a body continues in its state of rest or uniform motion unless acted upon by an unbalanced force.

INERTIA is the property of an object, including the body, which requires a force to unbalance it.

Consider this trick. Place a card over the mouth of a glass. On the card place a coin. Flick the card away and the coin drops into the glass.

With a little practice, you can even do this trick over a finger-tip.

But what will happen if you remove the card slowly? The coin will go with it.

When you are in stable equilibrium, e.g., standing in one of the stances, the inertia of your body tends to keep you stationary. To move you or overthrow you, this inertia has to be overcome. Time plays a part too. It takes a certain time to overcome the inertia. The shorter the time, the less effect there is to the stability.

That is why we always talk about speed when delivering a blow particularly a kick when the body is supported only by one leg. Not only that the blow is more likely to get home and less likely to be blocked but also that the stability is least disturbed. To benefit further from this property of inertia, we also talk about recovering the attacking limb immediately after impact so that the body regains its stable position quickly (centre of gravity within base area) and allows no time for the inertia to be overcome.

If you are in motion, inertia also tends to keep you in motion. If a bus driver suddenly stops the bus, the passengers will feel that their bodies continue to move forward. Depending on how fast you are moving, you may not be able to stop all at once. In combat situations, this should be taken into account when there is a lot of running and chasing. One general rule is not to strike when your opponent is running away from you but to strike when he is coming at you. Similarly, avoid plunging into an incoming blow. If you cannot stop yourself at once or block successfully.

The magnitude of inertia depends on the MASS of the body. The greater the

mass, the greater is the inertia.

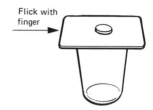

Flick with finger

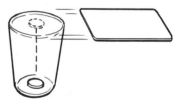

The law of acceleration

This law can be represented simply by the equation

$F = ma$ where

$\quad\quad\quad\quad\quad$ F = force exerted
$\quad\quad\quad\quad\quad$ m = mass
$\quad\quad\quad\quad\quad$ a = acceleration

i.e., Force = mass x acceleration

Imagine yourself falling off a stool. You may land safely. If you fall off the roof of your house, you may kill yourself. Why such difference? In both cases, the mass is the same, i.e., that of your body. Then the force difference is the result of acceleration. A certain interval of time is required to fall from the roof to the ground. The earth's gravitational attraction accelerates you all the time so that you are falling faster and faster for every moment passed. (The acceleration is 9·8 meters per second-per second meaning that for every second passed you are falling 9·8 meters faster than in the last second.) At the moment of impact, the acceleration is great enough to create a fatal force.

A bullet has a small mass. But its velocity is very high. Therefore its impact is terrific. A big rock may roll down the hill very slowly but its big mass can cause a damaging impact.

You may consider your hands and feet to have a constant mass. So now the equation becomes

Force = constant x acceleration.

Obviously, the way to get a greater force is to increase the acceleration. Arithmetically,

if $10 = 5 \times 2$

to get 15, the 2 has to be increased to 3, $15 = 5 \times 3$

similarly,
$$20 = 5 \times 4$$
$$25 = 5 \times 5 \text{ etc.}$$

Very often, a punch or a kick starts from a state of rest with zero velocity, e.g., the fist in ready position. This fist has to be sent to travel a certain distance within a certain time to hit the target. The theory of a blow is that from the initial velocity of zero, the fist (or foot) is to be continuously accelerated so that AT THE MOMENT OF IMPACT the acceleration is maximum. Then the force is maximum.

Further, acceleration is defined as the rate of change of velocity.

$$\text{acceleration} = \frac{\text{final velocity} - \text{initial velocity}}{\text{time taken}}$$

i.e., $a = \dfrac{V_f - V_i}{t}$

Now the equation becomes $F = m \dfrac{V_f - V_i}{t}$

To get maximum force, the general rule is then to accelerate to maximum final velocity in as short a time as possible.

The law of interaction
It states that for every action there is an equal and opposite reaction.

Once a little boy came to me and declared that he was going to hit me. I accepted the punishment, held out my fist and invited him to carry out the execution. He clenched his fist and hammered down at mine. After a couple of times, he stopped and exclaimed, 'Oh, that hurts!' We had a good laugh because we were not fighting. We were just playing.

That demonstrates the theory of a strike which is to connect a hard part of your anatomy to a soft part of your opponent's.

One last word
Now the book has come to an end. For you this is the beginning. May I wish you good luck and good health.